THE CANADIAN NON-PROFIT SECTOR

THE CANADIAN NON-PROFIT SECTOR

Neoliberalism and the Assault on Community

TED RICHMOND & JOHN SHIELDS

FERNWOOD PUBLISHING
HALIFAX AND WINNIPEG

Copyright 2024 © Ted Richmond and John Shields

All rights reserved. No part of this book may be reproduced or transmitted in any form by any means without permission in writing from the publisher, except by a reviewer, who may quote brief passages in a review.

Development editor: Errol Sharpe
Copyediting and text design: Brenda Conroy
Cover design: John van der Woude
Printed and bound in the UK

Published by Fernwood Publishing
Halifax and Winnipeg
2970 Oxford Street, Halifax, Nova Scotia, B3L 2W4
www.fernwoodpublishing.ca

Fernwood Publishing Company Limited gratefully acknowledges the financial support of the Government of Canada through the Canada Book Fund and the Canada Council for the Arts. We acknowledge the Province of Manitoba for support through the Manitoba Publishers Marketing Assistance Program and the Book Publishing Tax Credit. We acknowledge the Nova Scotia Department of Communities, Culture and Heritage for support through the Publishers Assistance Fund.

Library and Archives Canada Cataloguing in Publication
Title: The Canadian non-profit sector : neoliberalism and the assault on community / Ted Richmond &
John Shields.
Names: Richmond, Ted, author. | Shields, John, 1954- author.
Description: Includes bibliographical references and index.
Identifiers: Canadiana 20240355482 | ISBN 9781773636696 (softcover)
Subjects: LCSH: Nonprofit organizations‚ÄîCanada. | LCSH:
Neoliberalism‚ÄîCanada.
Classification: LCC HD2769.2.C3 R53 2024 | DDC 361.7/630971‚Äîdc23

This book is dedicated to all who work in the community non-profit sector. Their energy, commitment, and resourcefulness are crucial to the provision of essential health and social services and building community empowerment and citizen engagement.

Acknowledgements

We want to recognize all the student researchers and interns who have helped with our research and writing over the years (you know who you are). Special thanks as well to Hya Ali for her invaluable assistance with formatting the final version of the manuscript. Hya is a masters of public policy and administration student at Toronto Metropolitan University and a researcher with the Building Migrant Resilience SSHRC project attached to York University. We would also like to thank the Department of Politics and Public Administration at Toronto Metropolitan University for helping to fund the index for this volume. We also want to acknowledge the invaluable role of Errol Sharpe and the Fernwood team in the creative design and efficient production of this book.

Contents

Foreword 1

1 **The Non-profit Sector in Neoliberal Times** 4
   Precarity and Resilience 7
   Aims of the Volume 8
   Setting the Context 9
   Neoliberalism and the Non-profit Sector 10
   New Public Management 12
   Neoliberalism and Civil Society 14
   Neoliberalism's Impacts on Nonprofits 16
   A Critical Political Economy Perspective 17
   Bringing It All Together 19

2 **The Architecture of a Mission-Based Sector** 22
   What Is a Nonprofit? 22
   Architecture of the Non-profit Sector 25
   National Survey of Non-profit and Voluntary Organizations 26
   State of the Sector Report Ontario 28
   More Recent Data from Statistics Canada 32
   Other Organizations Linked to the Non-profit Sector 33
   Putting the Pieces Together 41

3 **Financial and Human Resources in
    the Non-profit Sector** 45
   A Vital Part of the Canadian Economy 46
   General Non-profit Financial Resources 46
   Donations as a Source of Funding 47
   Social Finance and Social Impact Bonds 51
   Human Resources 56
   Precarious Labour and the Contract Funding Regime 62
   Resilience in the Face of Adversity 68

4	**The Essential Role of Non-profit Advocacy**	**69**
	The Voluntary Sector Initiative	71
	Regulation of Charitable Activities and Advocacy Chill	77
	The Many Faces and Forms of Non-profit Advocacy	81
	Indigenous Rights	85
	Non-profit Advocacy Will Not Be Curtailed	89
5	**2020: A Year of Turbulence**	**91**
	Impact of the Pandemic	91
	Solidarity with Antiracist Struggles and Indigenous Rights	102
	Lessons Learned and Looking to the Future	107
6	**Future Challenges and Opportunities**	**110**
	Complex and Contradictory Relationships	110
	Into the Future	114
	Conclusion	120
Bibliography		**121**
Index		**136**

Foreword

Having moved to Toronto from Spain many years ago, my pathway into the non-profit sector started with a university friend, tired of hearing me whine that I missed speaking Spanish and telling me to look for volunteer work. I took that advice literally, found the Centre for Spanish-Speaking Peoples, and the rest is history, so to speak, in terms of my engagement in the sector. I did do volunteer work — interpreting for law students doing refugee hearings for Chileans, then Salvadorians; I was eventually hired under a student work experience initiative, and when I graduated with my masters in political science, I joined the staff collective as the legal secretary. I quickly progressed to being the coordinator of the centre, which was the ultimate generalist role. I supported the board of directors, led staff meetings, prepared budgets and funding applications, met with funders, helped plan and deliver programs, registered fee-paying students in our Spanish language classes (a budding social enterprise), managed volunteers, got involved in various advocacy and change initiatives, and finally, every day made sure there was toilet paper in the washrooms and took an occasional shift on reception.

Interestingly, my experience is not unique, even to this day, when you consider that over 90% of non-profits in Canada still operate with budgets of under $2–3 million. I am currently the executive director of Access Alliance, a community health centre working with newcomers, refugees, and people with precarious status — we prioritize those communities that have been made most vulnerable due to significant systemic barriers to social determinants of health. I am also part-time faculty at the Schulich School of Business at York University, where I teach a course on management issues in the non-profit sector.

I was lucky that early on in my professional trajectory I met people like Ted Richmond and John Shields. Based on their keen interest in the non-profit sector and critical focus on the larger context within which nonprofits were navigating, they practised collaborative knowledge creation and knowledge mobilization long before these became accepted and expected practices in research and sector building. John has always been an important academic voice and supporter concerning equitable access to settlement services and community advocacy. Ted has a long history as an activist, data enthusiast, researcher, and policy analyst in community, academic, and government institutions. Ted was an unofficial mentor to me and after a certain point in our relationship we would meet at least once a year for lunch, where he'd catch me up on his thinking. This was often linked to some collaboration with John, and he'd always leave me with some new insight to ponder until next time. Ted was also a volunteer for many years at Access Alliance, where he helped inform our vision for our community-based research program; he was instrumental in our establishing a support network and fellowship program for under-employed internationally trained researchers.

In my career I have experienced first-hand the consequences of polices of retrenchment, the downloading of government services onto community agencies, the erosion of grant funding and introduction of competitive tendering of contracts, increased scrutiny and regulation of the sector, the growth and at the same time the weakening of non-profit organizations due to inexorable increase in demand for services, and the non-profit starvation cycle. Canada's social deficit[1] exists as a result of growing income inequality, the emergence of precarious employment, transitional needs of immigrants and refugees, jurisdictional politics and lack of investment in the non-profit sector despite it being increasingly positioned as the solution to social inequities. For many years I believed that if we could just run better, smarter organizations, we could fix some of these problems. That was one of my motivations for returning to school, mid-career, to get my mba at the Schulich School of Business. I wasn't wrong but I wasn't right either, as I eventually realized.

John and Ted employ a critical political economy lens to understanding the forces at play in the evolution and positioning of the sector in our society. Characterizing the marketization of the provision of public goods and services as an assault on community, they examine the resilience of nonprofits within this neoliberal restructuring of Canada's economy and society. This volume unpacks the social, political, and economic forces at play, the role of nonprofits in advocacy, which

---

1 https://www.imaginecanada.ca/en/360/impact-emerging-social-deficit-charities-and-non-profits-infographic

the authors recognize to be equal in importance to human services in the missions of non-profits and give due attention to anti-Black racist mobilization and struggles for Indigenous rights among other issues related to equity and inclusion. The critical role of human resources, including volunteers, is also addressed.

Their analysis reminds us continually, and correctly, that these dynamics can only be understood in terms of the broader philosophy of gradually but relentlessly replacing government-funded essential health and human services with underfunded dependence on a volatile funding system and insecure and exploited contract labour. This book provides an overview of the many components of Canada's non-profit sector, including not just community-based health and social services, but also philanthropic foundations, cooperatives, advocacy organizations, and the "social economy" in Quebec. Of interest to a diverse audience and critical sectoral stakeholders, those who read this book will find it a significant contribution to our understanding of the vital role of Canada's non-profits, as well as the ongoing challenges they face.

— AXELLE JANCZUR
Executive Director, Access Alliance
Part-time faculty, Schulich School of Business, York University

CHAPTER 1

The Non-profit Sector in Neoliberal Times

This book is about the place of the non-profit sector in neoliberal times in Canada. Most of us may have only a vague idea of the non-profit sector and little sense of its significance. Yet, in our everyday lives we frequently encounter and engage with organizations that are part of this large and dynamic sector. We very likely do not even think of these bodies as nonprofits as they are such a regular part of our routines and activities. We may start our day by going to the gym at the YMCA. On the way to the Y we pass a homeless shelter. Our spouse starts their day by dropping our young daughter off at a community-based childcare facility before heading off to their job as a counsellor at a refugee centre. At lunchtime we have an appointment at a community health centre, where we pass a woman from the Salvation Army with a seasonal collection pot raising funds to help the needy. After school our child participates in a volunteer-run sports program at our neighbourhood community centre. Arriving home for dinner we see a member of the Victorian Order of Nurses leaving after a check-in visit to our elderly neighbour. The newspaper we read in the evening has three stories that catch our attention. The first is about the dramatic rise in food bank use due to the consequences of high inflation, which has expanded food insecurity well beyond the usual marginal population. The second story is about a coalition of environmental groups holding a protest in opposition to climate change at city hall. And the third item involves Black Lives Matters' strategy on confronting racism. We end the evening with a conversation regarding an upcoming meeting of our neighbourhood association.

Our day has been full of encounters with non-profit organizations and their activities. This brief scenario reflects how much the non-profit sector touches our lives and gives us a sense of the scope of organizations that are part of the sector. This non-profit "work grows out of community needs" (ONN 2023) embedded deeply in the local spaces where we live, work and engage in life-fulfilling activities.

The non-profit sector is composed of mission-driven organizations that are independent and not part of the formal state, and they are not profit-seeking entities. Any money they generate is put back into the organization and toward the missions they were created to address. In Chapter 2 we address the broad range of terms used to describe the sector and the organizations that comprise it. Throughout this volume, we use the terms non-profit (adjective) and nonprofit (noun). The adjective not-for-profit is also commonly used in the literature on the sector.

Given the broad range of organizations associated with the non-profit sector, what precisely falls within its boundaries is not clearly settled and consequently is subject to some variation depending upon who is employing the term. Thus, there is some fuzziness and often confusion among the public with respect to what is, and is not, within its scope. For example, there are 1) overlapping categories, as in the case of charities versus non-profit organizations (all charities are non-profits, but not all nonprofits are charities); 2) stretched boundaries, as in the cases of social enterprises run by nonprofits and cooperatives and credit unions, which are part of the larger social economy and operate in parallel with the private market economy; and 3) agencies that receive the bulk of their funding to provide services from government but which are organizationally constituted within a non-profit structure outside of government.

The separation between what is government versus nonprofit versus private market is particularly important for untangling what a non-profit organization is. The distinction can be seen in the following illustration. Governments in Canada provide funding for childcare in a variety of ways. Governments can transfer money directly to parents, giving them the "freedom" to purchase daycare services directly from private, for-profit childcare providers. Such services are part of the private market sector, even when all or part of the funding for this service comes from government. Alternatively, parents may choose to purchase services from a local mission-driven organization established on a not-for-profit basis. This organization and its services are part of the non-profit sector. Governments could also set up and run their own childcare facilities as part of direct state services (part of the government sector). So, services that are funded in whole or in part by government may be delivered through different segments of society — private market, non-profit or government sectors. Governments often "partner" with non-profit providers in the delivery of government-funded services. These complex relationships are more deeply examined in this volume. Later in the book we provide a formal definition of the non-profit sector and sketch its dimensions and scope in much greater detail, but you can already see the importance of non-profit organizations in our lives.

It is important to understand the broader context in which institutions like non-profit organizations come into our lives and the role they play in society. That broader context is neoliberalism. Neoliberalism has profoundly impacted our lives, including shaping the contemporary non-profit sector. That society has become increasingly reliant on the charitable work of food banks and homeless shelters speaks to the increasing influence of neoliberalism.

The term "neoliberalism" is used so frequently that some observers believe it is losing its meaning. But it remains essential to understand and acknowledge the impact of neoliberalism, both as ideology and as social policy. As an ideology, neoliberalism promotes the "logic" of replacing the social welfare support and protections of the state with the "efficiency" of a reliance on market forces and individual survival efforts. As social policy, neoliberalism works gradually but relentlessly to reduce social benefits, public economic supports, and universal health care. This policy approach has greatly deepened inequalities in society, fostering widespread social exclusion (Richmond and Saloojee 2005). Individuals, families, and non-profit organizations are expected to be responsible for addressing more and more of the problems faced in an increasingly polarized society.

Consequently, the non-profit sector is left to fill the many gaps created by a state retreating from its social responsibilities and supports. Non-profit organizations act as a backup for when the state fails to address pressing social and economic problems like homelessness, rent poverty, and food insecurity. But, as we discuss later, the non-profit sector has limited capacities to deal with such profound challenges. This volume seeks to provide a deeper understanding of the non-profit sector and its roles in an environment dominated by neoliberalism.

Precarity and Resilience

Like the ancient Roman god Janus, the contemporary non-profit sector presents two faces: on the one side the sector is characterized as precarious, but on the other it is presented as resilient. This seeming contradiction is useful for understanding the inherent dynamics of the sector in the age of neoliberalism. This duality is actually part of the dynamic tension amplified by the process of neoliberal restructuring. Hence, precarity/resilience is a useful dichotomy by which to explore and understand the non-profit sector and the crosscutting pressures that it confronts. While the themes of precarity and resilience do not fully encompass the full range of subject matter we cover in this book, they are valuable as an overall framework for analysis.

Briefly, precarity relates to the state of persistent uncertainty and insecurity. This is often associated with precarious employment, a major problem found in the non-profit sector itself (Procyk, Lewchuk, and Shields 2017). Precariousness extends well beyond employment, however, and is more widely experienced through society, such as in the cases of health, housing, and food insecurities. Organizations themselves can be precarious, as many nonprofits have to deal with the persistent problem of funding insecurity (Shields, Cunningham, and Baines 2017). And non-profit sector missions are also often directed toward addressing precarity-related problems within society that are growing deeper.

Resilience is about the ability to bounce back and recover from adversity. It involves the capacity to adapt and adjust to difficult circumstances. While resilience is often applied to individual capacities, it also relates to organizations and larger systems, including non-profit organizations (Wiig and Fahlbrunch 2019). The ability of non-profit organizations to regularly innovate in order to "do more with less" is a resilient characteristic found in the sector. There are, however, different approaches to the idea of resilience. Neoliberal notions of resilience are reactive and limited. For the non-profit sector, neoliberal resilience is often about non-profit organizations' abilities to manage through their precarity, or, in the words of Leary (2018, 151), to "resiliently endure." While non-profit organizations struggle in the face of neoliberal restructuring and precarity, this often results in limited neoliberal-oriented resilient responses. Broader and more progressive conceptions of resilience speak to not only an ability to deal with adversity, survival, and recovery but to transform — to build back better (Preston, Shields, and Akbar 2022). The social justice missions of many non-profit organizations provide the fuel for transformative resilience. These two contrasting neoliberal and more progressive resilience forces are ever present in the operational lives of non-profit organizations. Thus, the concepts of precarity and resilience are helpful for unpacking the dynamics of the non-profit sector in a time of neoliberal change.

Aims of the Volume

This book presents a broad overview of the non-profit sector in Canada, with relevant statistics as available. There is a strong focus on the part of the non-profit sector that provides social, human, and health services because of their vital role in Canada's changing welfare state system and community well-being. The evolution of this non-profit role under neoliberalism dramatically highlights the challenges and tensions faced by the non-profit sector as a whole.

The overall effect of neoliberal restructuring has been to leave individuals and families scrambling for survival and to leave the underfunded and over-administered non-profit sector to try to patch over the steadily growing fissures in our society. One example of the destructive impact of neoliberalism on community organizations is the transition of government support over the past decades in Canada from *program funding* to limited and precarious *project funding* — creating perpetual financial insecurity and permanent administrative overload. Another result, directly related to project funding, is the "permanently temporary" employment status of most staff in the sector.

Project funding is aimed toward a specific output, with directed objects to be completed over a defined timeframe (often one to three years). For example, a project may be aimed at employment training for individuals on social assistance, with specific targets of numbers of clients "successfully" employed at the end and hence off welfare rolls. The funding for such projects is short term and tied to narrowly defined "successful" outcomes. By contrast, program funding is more broadly focused on larger themes, for example, a program aimed at achieving full employment in quality work. This is a long-term goal, involving many projects tied to more open-ended, secure, multi-year funding (Alonzi n.d.). Neoliberalism, as noted, has seen a decisive movement away from program funding for nonprofits to project-based funding.

Another important theme of the book is the diversity of the sector, something not adequately reflected in statistics or current analysis. We also examine the issue of advocacy as one of the essential functions of the sector and as a revealing lens into the dynamics of relations between the state (including its funding branches) and the voices of communities. Finally, to further reveal the precariousness and resilience of the sector and the contradictions posed by neoliberalism, we consider the response of the non-profit sector to recent upheavals: the COVID-19 pandemic crisis and the emergence of anti-Black racism and Indigenous rights as issues capturing their rightful claim to serious public consideration.

The non-profit sector covers a vast terrain, and we do not set out to examine in detail all the different components and aspects of the sector and the organizations that make it up. Rather, we seek to offer a comprehensible understanding of the sector in neoliberal times. Overall, consequently, the purpose of this volume is to provide a digestible and critical understanding of the non-profit sector. This book is designed to be accessible to a broad audience composed of students, academics, public interest readers, non-profit practitioners, and the broader public policy community. This work is inherently cross-disciplinary and suitable for social science-based courses ranging from political science and sociology to social work and community services. Senior undergraduate through to graduate courses will find this subject matter to be of added value for introducing and situating this understudied sector to their own subject area. The compact length of the book makes it a desirable companion volume for course adoption.

Setting the Context

Over the past two decades or so, the non-profit sector in Canada and elsewhere has moved from relative obscurity into the mainstream of public life. In fact, thirty years ago there was considerable questioning as to whether a non-profit sector even existed (Laforest 2011b). Today, nonprofits have been thrust into the centre of public policy debate and become widely used by governments as instruments in public policy. Nonprofits are being asked to do ever more in society as the state retreats in terms of its roles and responsibilities. The vital importance of studying the non-profit sector lies in its increasing relevance to societal well-being in the context of growing inequality and the ever-shrinking social provision offered directly by government.

The non-profit sector has become centrally positioned in the so-called "great risk shift" (Hacker 2019), as the state's role in protecting and supporting society against a host of risks — economic, social, and health insecurities, environmental hazards, housing and transportation poverty, and much more — have been transferred away from government onto individuals, families, and communities (Beck 1992). As civil society organizations, nonprofits have been left to provide as best they can what is, essentially, a thinned-out insecure layer of supports to help mitigate such risks.

The purposes and roles of non-profit organizations are multi-dimensional, but their two main objectives are to provide services in support of their mission and to engage in mission-based advocacy. Hence, their roles as both service and "voice"-centred institutions are well recognized and fundamental. Strongly connected to the voice role is the place non-profit organizations play in civil society and in the enhancement of democratic forces in society. Independent organizations with strong voices, rooted in communities, are crucial to strong democracies. The muting of such voices by the operation of neoliberalism represents a profound threat to the health of democratic society. Robert Putnam (2000), for one, links the crisis of civic democracy to the decline in participation in public-facing non-profit organizations. This decline coincides with the rise of neoliberalism as the dominant policy paradigm and as the new societal "common sense."

Neoliberalism and the Non-profit Sector

The non-profit sector is a dynamic entity, with many resilient characteristics, operating in an environment increasingly shaped by neoliberal marketization. The pressure of neoliberal restructuring has directly influenced the structure, operational nature, and cultural ethos of non-profit organizations. This has a profound impact on the kind of services offered and the way such services are provided, the accountability for funding dollars and outcomes, the basic mission orientation, and the kinds of voice and types of advocacy undertaken. It is essential, therefore, to employ a critical lens when examining the non-profit sector and to look at the role and operation of nonprofits within a broader and changing societal context.

Neoliberalism arose in the 1970s out of a crisis of capitalism. Thirty years of post–World War II economic expansion and a rapid increase in affluence among broad bodies of the population in the "developed" industrial countries was abruptly upended by both rapidly rising unemployment and inflation — a phenomenon called stagflation. Stagflation, the coexistence of high rates of unemployment and inflation, under the logic of Keynesian economics was thought not to be possible as unemployment and inflation were said to be economic forces that offset one another — high unemployment was to have a dampening effect on inflation and vice versa.

Stagflation was propelled by an oil crisis brought on by the Arab-Israeli War of 1973, which greatly disrupted economies and created artificially high prices for an essential commodity whose price a slowing economy was not able to moderate. The crisis was spurred on by global economic restructuring, with Western nations experiencing a process of "deindustrialization." As industrial production shifted to the developing world, previously prosperous blue-collar communities in the West became economically hollowed-out "rust-belt" regions. This set of fundamental upheavals undermined the previous political consensus rooted in Keynesian public policy. A policy window was opened, which neoliberal ideas and policy prescriptions passed through to become the dominant political and social forces in society (McBride and Shields 1997; Burke, Mooers, and Shields 2000).

Neoliberalism promotes a more limited role for the state in public provision and a greatly enhanced role for markets and individual "freedom" for consumers and entrepreneurs. Market exchanges and contractual relations are viewed as the basis for all forms of human action as they are believed to maximize individual freedom and initiative and produce optimal economic benefit — principally the freedom to act in the marketplace. Marketization and privatization are seen as the route to achieving such neoliberal goals. Neoliberalism embraces a kind of religion of pure market principles. This is part of the risk shift transferred down onto communities, families, and individuals in terms of managing their own well-being, thus creating greater insecurity and societal precarity. This neoliberal process is referred to as "responsibilization" (Kelly and Caputo 2011).

Marketization demands that market criteria be used in the provision of public goods and resources, which tend to focus on human capital investment to enhance the competitive position of the state. Privatization calls upon the state to withdraw from the provision of goods and services.

Government may still be involved in funding "public" services[1] in more austere ways, but the provider is to be located increasingly outside the state — in particular, with non-profit service providers. This is a highly disruptive process, resulting in challenging and painful adjustments and crises throughout society, including within the non-profit sector itself (Joy and Shields 2020). The distancing of the state from direct provision of public services is leading to the hollowing out of the welfare state. The process shields the neoliberal state from clear public view in terms of its place in reducing its financial commitments to programs.

New Public Management

For the social, human, and health component of nonprofits, neoliberalism came to the sector most prominently through new public management (NPM). NPM was part of the neoliberal "reinventing government" movement of the later 1980s and 1990s (Osborne and Gaebler 1992). A key goal was to shrink the size of the state, in part by embracing alternative service delivery (ASD), in which non-profit service organizations would become the main delivery agents of government programs and services. To reinvent and shrink the state, government would need to steer — focus on policy setting and coordination — and leave the rowing — the actual delivery of services — as much as possible to other agencies (Osborne and Gaebler 1992). This logic led to a central place for non-profit service providers within neoliberal governance practice.

The neoliberal state has cast its approach as one of "shared governance" and "partnership," but NPM's real aim is to place power in the hands of the neoliberal state in order to control the overall direction of neoliberal restructuring, including the restructuring of the non-profit sector itself (Shields and Evans 1998). The benign language of shared governance and partnership masks the hierarchical power structured into the contractual relationship that NPM imposes between the state and non-profit service providers.

According to the neoliberal paradigm, only the market is able to deliver efficiency and effectiveness; hence the private sector business model is the best path for the production of all goods and services (Evans 2020). Bringing this market mechanism into the public sector by the

---

1   Government services are, of course, non-profit but they are determined by politically driven processes. In the non-profit sector the organizations come from civil society and their non-profit orientation is mission based.

adoption of a purchaser–provider split was made a reality through ASD and its management under NPM. This enforced competitive tendering and contracting on nonprofits, generating a market-like framework. The market efficiency and economic discipline imposed on non-profit providers pushes risk onto them and away from the neoliberal state (Walsh 1995, 26). This increased risk and loss of autonomy to the neoliberal state places non-profit providers into precarious positions.

As noted, NPM is the prime way that neoliberal ideas and practices are transferred to the non-profit sector. In this regard, NPM acts as a transmission belt for neoliberalism in the non-profit sector. Two basic elements make up NPM — managerialism and modes of control (Shields and Evans 1998).

The core aspect of managerialism concerns the professional management direction of organizations with an emphasis on "managers' rights to manage." This private sector business-based orientation regarding how non-profit organizations are expected to operate in the delivery of government-funded services reinforces hierarchical managerial authority, in opposition to a more grassroots, community-centred approach.

Modes of control are about the process of "centralized decentralization" — indirect control — as a way for the funder to manage from a distance. This seemingly contradictory idea allows the neoliberal state to decentralize the delivery of services while at the same time still controlling delivery operations through the terms of the government's funding contracts. Directed by NPM, non-profit service providers must bend to neoliberal accountability systems (Ascoli and Ranci 2002). The neoliberal state, using competitive service contracts and their strict rules of adherence to contract terms, is able to control how nonprofits provide their services and to whom. Hence, the neoliberal state effectively controls most aspects of contracted non-profit service provision from a distance to realize the goal of "centralized decentralization."

Consequently, while the neoliberal state "shrinks" in size, it simultaneously enhances its power and control. The state's "leaning" process is about trimming its so-called fat by realigning the state's role in society. It is not about weakening the state. Andrew Gamble (1988) characterized neoliberalism as about the "strong state and free economy." Under neoliberalism, social welfare supports shrink, the economy is deregulated, and the coercive powers of the state are enhanced to enforce greater social control and a law-and-order agenda.

The operation of NPM promotes a one-sided accountability framework directed upward toward the funder, and in particular the government funder. However, accountability in the non-profit sector is in reality multi-directional: downward to clients and communities; lateral to non-profit boards, agency workers, volunteers, and community partners; and, upward, of course, to funders. NPM and market logic have worked to diminish the more community- and grassroots-oriented accountability approaches in favour of a market/funder-centred accountability system consistent with "centralized decentralization" (Richmond and Shields 2005; Evans and Shields 2014).

Another aspect of ASD through contract financing is that the government funder does not pay the full value of the costs to the non-profit organization for delivering the service. It has been estimated that there is up to a 15% shortfall in operating budgets for such services. Nonprofits are expected to make up this funding gap with volunteer labour, donations, and "doing more with less" (Eakin 2007, 14–16; 2002, 8). This places non-profit providers in a perpetual state of precarity, producing fiscal stress and capacity deficits (Shields and Abu Alrob 2021).

Neoliberalism and Civil Society

Neoliberalism also impacts nonprofits by generating forces that disorganize civil society (Jäger 2022). Civil society constitutes the space between the state, the market, and the family. It provides the breathing space where formal and informal associations occur and can flourish to create societal bonds that allow for community formation, the nurturing of community spirit, and action promoting community health and well-being within broadly inclusive communities. This stands in contrast to the atomistic (hyper individualist) orientation of the market sphere and neoliberalism. For Robert Ware (1999, 307), the contrast between the values found in communities of civil society versus markets are substantive:

> Communities are the place for public moral activity, while markets are the place for private [for profit] activity. Communities, at their best, foster recognition, care and co-operation. Communities are considered the place for openness, security and trust. Markets are places for secrecy, insecurity and distrust.... Communities look for dignity and

equality. Markets look for fitness and success.... The problem is that our society is awash with markets but in need of substantive community with public values.

By marketizing and imposing neoliberal values in all parts of society, including civil society, the values of community are undermined.

Non-profit organizations are a core component of broader civil society; they are in fact considered the organizational face of civil society and community (Fumkin 2009). For Michael Edwards (2004, 14), non-profit organizations embody society's "reservoir of caring, cultural life and intellectual innovation," which constitute the building blocks of resilience and community formation.

Neoliberalism, however, poses a direct threat to the health of civic society and community due to its championing of the cult of markets and extreme individualism above all else. As Anto Jäger (2022, 52) observes: "Individualization was imperative for capital, and collective life had to be diminished in order for the market to find new avenues for accumulation [profit]." This has resulted in decreasing involvement and membership in non-profit organizations. Robert Putnam (2000) speaks of this as the "bowling alone" phenomenon. People are still bowling but increasingly not in leagues, rather as individuals and/or with an isolated friend or family member, greatly weakening wider networks that foster social bonds. Putnam documents the dramatic decline in membership in a vast array of civic organizations in North America. As Jäger (2022, 52) notes: "Far beyond the bowling alley, social life in the West had indeed become increasingly atomistic."

Christopher Lasch (1995) adds that the rise of a highly atomized society works to undermine the idea of "the 'common life' and renders the world instead 'a war of all against all'" — a world where the priority is one of self-interest and survival (Lorentzen 2022, 23), like the description of the operation of individuals in the free marketplace offered by Ware. This is a largely asocial existence where the wealthy wall themselves off in privately protected gated spaces, distancing themselves from the precarious others (Lasch 1995). It creates "a wasteland of sociability" (Jäger 2022, 51), growing loneliness, unhappiness, isolation, and extreme expressions of individualism — an increasingly asocial order where conspiracy theories, racism, and anti-immigrant attitudes thrive (Lauer, Wong, and Yan 2022, 5). In a society dominated by neoliberal values, the role of nonprofits in helping to deepen citizenship, participation, social cohesion, and community has been greatly compromised.

Neoliberalism's Impacts on Nonprofits

The non-profit sector has been and continues to be on the frontlines of the neoliberal transformation of Canadian society. Thus, we can better understand many of the changes happening in society as a result of neoliberal shifts by observing their workings in the sector and their activities in the community. For example, the non-profit sector is a particularly effective site for examining the phenomenon of precarity, making clear its impacts on non-profit workers, non-profit organizations, vulnerable communities, and society as a whole.

In spite of these pressures and challenges, the non-profit sector in general and the service component in particular have continued to demonstrate remarkable resilience — often in the face of government-imposed obstacles. Through creativity, advocacy, and strategic partnerships, the sector has generally preserved and sometimes extended the minimum level of funding sufficient to maintain the most vital services.[2] Extensive and creative use of volunteers has helped maintain programs and the organizations themselves. Administrative efficiencies, improvements in reporting of activities, and the embrace of new technologies, such as online service delivery, have also boosted the resilience of the sector.

Throughout this process the sector has also continued to develop its advocacy for human rights and social justice, both in Canada and internationally, and to speak on behalf of the most vulnerable members of society. Of course, the resilience of the non-profit sector has been both demonstrated and tested during the COVID-19 pandemic. The precarious positioning of so many non-profit organizations has been a vivid demonstration of the limitations of the capacity of the sector. Contrary to the neoliberal position, the pandemic has also demonstrated the need to bring back the state as an active and progressive agent of social and economic support working in a collaborative way with the non-profit sector.

---

2   The impact of the COVID-19 pandemic and the associated instability of funding, including donations, is examined later in this book.

A Critical Political Economy Perspective

Although the non-profit sector is under-studied, in spite of its vital role in Canadian society, important contributions to the study of this sector have been made by a relatively small number of academics and researchers. We recognize this and cite much of this vital input extensively. At the same time, however, much that is written about the sector reflects a limited and mainstream perspective that is often misleading or even flawed (Coule, Dodge, and Eikenberry 2022). Some authors, for example, write from a technical vantage point, often informed by a "new public administration/governance" perspective (Pestoff, Brandsen, and Verschuere 2011). This viewpoint speaks to the role of the sector in advancing alternative service delivery, enabling government to shrink in size and improve the so-called "efficiency" of public service through the application of business-oriented management. It also focuses on a marketized relationship between state-funded services and programs and their clients, in contrast to deeper notions of state-citizenship relationships that have been compromised by commodified relationships (Evans and Shields 2018).

Another prominent stream of the literature is influenced by a US-centric perspective (Salamon 1999) that rather uncritically embraces liberal individualism and the value of voluntarism. This framework is embodied in the notion that a thriving non-profit sector in the US provides the foundations of democracy and liberty, serving as a bulwark against the perceived threats of big government and state bureaucracy. This stream of thought stretches back to the early nineteenth-century French commentator Alexis de Tocqueville, who pointed to the "unique" American phenomenon of the rise of thousands of civil society organizations to independently and spontaneously address community needs, a force forming the basis of American democracy (Ott 2001, 3). This approach also exists in some variants of communitarian thought that is anti-statist and views community as arising organically out of voluntarism and a network of non-profit organizations.

Yet another line of thought, prominently associated with business schools, embraces the values of entrepreneurialism, markets, and competition as the way forward for the non-profit sector. They promote the ability of the sector to use markets for achieving their mission goals, including social justice aims. This orientation also champions the positive place of philanthropy and corporate social responsibility for addressing the modern challenges of society, including growing socio-economic polarization and the spread of social exclusion. The *Stanford Social Innovation Review* is a prime example of this line of thought. The non-profit sector in general and philanthropy, in particular, are viewed as privileged sites of innovation and progress, marshalling the positive power of markets and enlightened self-interest (Guo and Bielefeld 2014). This perspective is contrasted with supposedly overly rigid government in a state of perpetual fiscal deficit and hence incapable of dealing with "wicked" or stubbornly difficult policy issues. Hence, entrepreneurial nonprofits and wealthy philanthropists are considered the ideal actors to address society's most pressing issues — a viewpoint that is strongly contested (Burgis 2022; McGoey 2015).

Another common perspective, widely shared among non-profit sector commentators, spokespersons, and practitioners, sees the sector as inherently progressive — "on the side of truth and justice" but crippled by restrictive government policies, an often uncaring or unaware public, and limited independent economic resources. The sector is cast, rather idealistically, as a force for good in a generally hostile world — one that requires only greater resources and less legislative restriction to lead progressive policy development. This positioning is often seen as a useful vantage point from which to advocate to government for more resources to fulfill their good works for society. There is much that is valid in this outlook, but it ignores the real and growing tensions within the sector, including significant disparities between larger and smaller organizations in financial assets and policy influence, competitive attitudes, and practices (often heightened by funding rules) and a degree of acquiescence to various direct and indirect restrictions on advocacy.

Further confusion comes from the ubiquitous practice of labelling the entire sector with terms that describe only a portion of its overlapping components. The term "voluntary sector" for example has been much favoured in the recent past, particularly by government funders who like to imagine that non-profit health and social service providers can expand their activities without additional funding. But the sector, despite its commitment to community service, is not essentially "voluntary." Much of its work and indeed its very survival rely on paid staff working along with volunteers, making it reliant in turn on adequate funding from government, supplemented by revenue generation and non-government grants. Equally misleading is the term "charitable sector," since a significant portion of sector organizations, especially the smaller social service organizations on the front lines in serving the most vulnerable, are not registered as charitable organizations.

None of the approaches or perspectives outlined above, therefore, fully reflect the complexities and contradictions of Canada's non-profit sector. We present instead in this book a critical approach that situates the contemporary non-profit sector in a historical context, within a process of political change, the marketization of society, and the trends toward enhanced inequality and dispossession and marginalization of the less powerful and less well off. Situating the non-profit sector and understanding its role in this process of neoliberal restructuring are at the centre of our analysis. Consequently, we employ a critical political economy framework that takes into consideration the contradictory dynamics at work within the sector but which also gives recognition to its progressive elements and potentialities, as well as its material limits.

Critical political economy (CPE) draws on a multidisciplinary approach. It takes into account the dynamics of unequal structures of power in shaping processes and outcomes, dynamics which involve social forces such as class, gender, race, ethnicity, and citizenship/immigration status. CPE recognizes that societal, political, and economic factors cannot be separated and need to be considered in relation to one another in a holistic manner (Joy and Shields 2020; Whiteside 2020). The approach recognizes that no analysis is value free and embraces a value-informed perspective rooted in social justice. But CPE also rejects idealistic positions, embedding its analysis within concrete material foundations.

Bringing It All Together

We view the non-profit sector as occupying a dialectical position within the process of neoliberal societal restructuring. On the one hand, the sector has been employed to facilitate neoliberal downloading, to in effect operate as a band-aid to cover growing social and economic gaps left by a retreating state. On the other hand, the sector is a source of resistance to neoliberalism, a sphere for the promotion of social justice and a voice for the community. These complex dynamics often lie in tension with one another.

The sector, for example, can be seen as providing a "safety net" to address social problems like poverty, homelessness, and food insecurity. In this way nonprofits help to legitimate the unequal structures created under capitalism. Joan Roelofs (1995) argues that, in fact, the non-profit sector serves as a "protective layer for capitalism," providing interim measures and stopgaps that contain forces of popular mobilization and resistance to capitalist market forces. The non-profit role in society can be seen as an important part of the "supports" addressing social gaps that assist in reinforcing the existing power structures by legitimating this highly inequitable system.

However, it is also the case that non-profit organizations can and do serve as agents of change. Many nonprofits engage in forceful and effective social justice advocacy organizing and in promoting policy and societal reform. In this way they function as "change agents" and facilitators of democratic engagement within civil society. Additionally, because non-profit organizations are often community-based and work to bring people together and help to forge connections, they function as bonding institutions that build social capital and can help to foster social inclusion. These are valuable contributions within society and one of the reasons nonprofits have come to be viewed as an important institution in building more stable and inclusive communities.

However, nonprofits have also been deliberately employed by the neoliberal state as organizations that help to displace the Keynesian welfare state, in their function as cheap or even free alternative "public" service providers. In this regard the non-profit sector serves the needs of the neoliberal austerity and anti-state agendas. Hence, the many facets of the sector must be taken into account in any comprehensive analysis, as we set out to do in this volume. This book probes broad questions such as: What role does the non-profit sector and non-profit voluntary activity play in a market-centred society? How have non-profit roles and efforts been affected and transformed by the forces of neoliberalism and the reshaped political economy of the non-profit sector itself? How does neoliberalism's ethic of individualism, aggressive pursuit of self-interest, and general faith in the logic and value system of a "markets know best" system of governance, fit with the sector's seemingly contradictory values, centred around ideas such as community, solidarity, sharing, reciprocity, and missions oriented toward the general good? Since neoliberal interest in the sector is centred on moving toward a more privatized system of welfare and transforming the non-profit sector along more marketized lines, what do we know about how far this agenda has progressed and the implications for the non-profit sector and society more generally? Does, or can, the non-profit sector offer an effective counter to such an agenda?

In the chapters that follow we address these questions and provide an overview of the shape and nature of the sector in the Canadian context, as well as addressing a number of key themes, including advocacy and the diversity of the sector. The next chapter provides an overview of the sector and Chapter 3 looks in more detail at its financial and human resources. Chapter 4 examines the crucial issue of advocacy by, and for, the sector. Chapter 5 gives a brief look at the still-developing impact on the sector of the COVID-19 pandemic and the associated instability of funding, including donations, and the growing public awareness of issues such as anti-Black racism and Indigenous rights. Finally, Chapter 6 summarizes our main findings and examines more closely the differing political and ideological perspectives revealed by our analysis.

CHAPTER 2

The Architecture of a Mission-Based Sector

In this chapter we present an overview of the non-profit sector in Canada. An outline of the architecture of the sector and its associated parts is vital to understanding the sector's size and scope and to placing it more fully within Canada's contemporary political economy. This chapter reveals the diversity of the sector and the broader dimensions of non-profit activity connected with the social economy. In order to consider the non-profit sector critically, its full material dimensions and associated elements must be established. We begin with a formal definition of a non-profit organization and identify the various roles and functions of the sector.

What Is a Nonprofit?

Most depictions of nonprofits try to capture their essence as being organizations that exist in that area between the private and state sectors — the hazy middle ground — and in this sense they are generally framed as what they are not — they do not pursue profit and they are not government agencies. This kind of depiction tends to marginalize nonprofits, minimizing their unique and important positioning in society. Given their important place in society, nonprofits are deserving of recognition as distinctive organizations performing vital roles. Lester Salamon and Helmut Anheir (1997) outline the following five common features of non-profit organizations:

1. Formally constituted — this can take many forms ranging from highly organized and formal organizations that are legally incorporated to very small organizations that are purely voluntary and much more informal but do engage in such activities as regular meetings. The great diversity of the non-profit sector

means there are wide-ranging differences in the organizational structures of organizations which make up the sector. What is common is that there exists some degree, even if loosely based, of ongoing organizational reality to their existence.

2. Institutionally separate from government — nonprofits are separate and independent bodies distinct from the state. This is not to say that nonprofits do not receive government funding and partner with the state, as many of them do. Some would claim that "dependence" of a nonprofit can result in state capture of the organization (a problem we discuss in relation to the neoliberalism and nonprofits), but formally speaking, nonprofit organizations remain distinct and separate entities from government with the capacity to make their own decisions.

3. Non-profit seeking — unlike private businesses the driving force behind non-profit organizations is not the pursuit of profit that is distributed to private interests in or outside the organization. Rather, the key distinguishing feature of nonprofits is that they are "mission-based" organizations.

> Mission orientation is, in a sense, the fundamental distinguishing characteristic of non-profit organizations. Where for-profit organizations acquire the organizational *raison d'être* fundamentally from the pursuit of profit, non-profit organizations get theirs from the pursuit of a mission, a purpose that binds the agency's personnel, supporters, and beneficiaries together in common purpose. (Salamon 1995, 217)

This is not to say that nonprofits do not engage in activities that generate income; they may even run a "social enterprise" (examined below), but all revenues from such sources are directed solely for the benefit of advancing the mission of the nonprofit and not to enriching private interests.

4. Self-governance — nonprofits are self-directed autonomous organizations. Non-profit management boards composed of volunteers direct the activities of most non-profit organizations.

5. Voluntary effort — there is a voluntary component to non-profit bodies. Most nonprofits to some degree or other make use of volunteers. But the amount of volunteerism employed varies considerably, given the diversity of organizations that

make up the sector. Some nonprofits, often smaller ones, are only composed of volunteers. Larger nonprofits, and in particular nonprofits in the social, human, and health service fields, may use mostly paid labour. This paid labour force is often more poorly compensated than workers in other sectors of the economy (see Chapter 3), and non-profit paid workers are often attracted to the sector due to its mission orientation even if more poorly compensated. The spirit of voluntary effort may be said to guide much of this paid workforce. At the very least, the boards of management that oversee non-profit organizations are solely voluntary bodies (this is a legal requirement).

The Organisation for Economic Co-operation and Development (OECD) characterizes the non-profit sector as

> a sector between the state and market, filling both economic and social missions, which pursues a general interest, and whose final objective is not the redistribution of profit. Each of these terms underlies only one aspect of the sector. (OECD 2003, 10)

The mission orientation of the sector stands out as the sector's most distinguishing feature. The sector is known for its values, which are embodied in such concepts as "the ethic of caring and giving," voluntarism, charity, philanthropy, altruism, mutuality, and reciprocity (Evans and Shields 2010, 305).

The two key roles of non-profit organizations are service and advocacy. The mission of nonprofits is "to do good works" (Cappe 1999, 2) by providing services to the community or their membership. These services are wide ranging and may be provided independently or in partnership with government. Advocacy (see detailed coverage in Chapter 4) is a central function of nonprofits as it contributes to democratic engagement, especially by providing avenues for the less powerful in society to become engaged in the political process and by amplifying their voices.

Additionally, non-profit organizations are often strategically located in society where they can play a mediating role. They are frequently able to bring together diverse interests from across a spectrum or a geographical area to work out differences and come to a consensus or compromise on issues. In this way nonprofits can play a positive role in facilitating social cohesion and social inclusion (Evans and Shields 2010, 307).

Nonprofits also contribute to building citizenship. This is because citizenship is fundamentally about participation in society as a whole — not just narrowly at the level of government (Evans and Shields 2010, 308). Nonprofits are about civic engagement, volunteering, and working together for common goals. The opportunities and activities opened by non-profit organizations help to stimulate working for active community membership and against passive, non-engaged notions of citizenship.

Architecture of the Non-profit Sector

We know the non-profit sector in Canada is large, diverse, and growing. Even limited statistics from various sources estimate that there are more than 170,000 incorporated non-profit organizations in Canada, with about half of these being registered charities (Barr 2021). An estimated 360 charities are added to the total each year, so the growth of nonprofits has been outpacing the growth of both the state and market sectors over the last number of decades (Emmett and Emmett 2015, 15; Imagine Canada n.d.).

Based on 2020 economic activity data, the non-profit sector contributed some $189 billion to the economy, representing 8.7% of Canada's gross domestic product (GDP) (Imagine Canada n.d.). The most significant portion of non-profit activity (73.2%) came from so-called government non-profit institutions, such as hospitals, universities, and community colleges. Community-centred non-profit institutions (the "core" sector) accounted for 16.4% of the overall sector, while business non-profit institutions accounted for 10.4% (Statistics Canada 2019b).

Most organizations in the core sector are small, with annual revenues below $100,000. But a significant number are larger, and these represent the bulk of the revenues and paid workforce in the core sector (Elson 2009). In addition, an even larger number (many times the number of formally organized non-profit organizations) are "below the radar" entities run totally by volunteers with extremely limited budgets. These organizations are quintessentially local and likely constitute the bulk of unreported voluntary activity; they are not captured by standard statistical surveys. This part of the sector also appears to be expanding (McCabe and Phillimore 2018). Hence, the contemporary non-profit sector is a substantive component of Canada's overall political economy.

Knowing or even estimating the full size and scope of the non-profit sector in Canada is challenging. It is difficult to accurately survey the many small organizations that compose a large part of the sector, as many are solely run by volunteers and not legally registered either as nonprofits or as charitable organizations. Another challenge is the paucity of good data — federal research on the sector has been limited and inconsistent,[1] and most provinces do not survey their sector organizations. Consequently, it is only registered charities that we have regular and reliable data about as these organizations are required by law to report to the Canada Revenue Agency (CRA) each year (Barr 2021). Given the size and economic importance of the non-profit sector in Canada, the "data deficit" in relation to its tracking is striking (Barr 2021; Jenson 2021). This data deficit has larger implications as it makes it difficult for the sector to demonstrate in numbers the full societal contribution and value of nonprofits to policymakers and state funders.

A review of the statistics that are available does, however, provide essential information about the size of the sector — allowing for undercounting of registered non-profit non-charities and other unregistered nonprofits — as well as the scope of its activities. Such a review also reveals much about the main component parts of the sector, and the similarities and differences with respect to their organizational forms and specialized activities. This can be approached both by comparing existing statistical data for the sector as a whole and through examination of some of the specialized reports and surveys from different non-profit sub-sectors.

National Survey of Non-profit and Voluntary Organizations

The National Survey of Non-profit and Voluntary Organizations (NSNVO) was the first comprehensive, pan-Canadian statistical survey of the non-profit sector in Canada. Conducted in 2003, the survey gathered data from 13,000 incorporated non-profit organizations, defined as follows: nongovernmental (institutionally separate from governments), non-profit-distributing (do not return any profits generated to their owners or directors), self-governing (are independent and able to regulate their own activities), voluntary (benefit to some considerable

---

1 The lack of federal initiative is related to factors such as the lack of follow up on the NSNVO associated with the Voluntary Sector Initiative (VSI) and the austerity-induced cuts at Statistics Canada under the Harper Conservative government, which limited its ability to conduct formal national surveys of the sector.

degree from voluntary contributions of time or money), and formally incorporated or registered under specific legislation with provincial, territorial, or federal governments (Statistics Canada 2004). The scope of the NSNVO excluded grassroots organizations and citizens' groups that were not formally incorporated or registered with provincial, territorial, or federal governments, as well as some registered charities considered to be public sector agencies, such as school boards, public libraries, and public schools.

The summary findings of the NSNVO from Statistics Canada[2] reported that the story of non-profit and voluntary organizations is one of Canadians coming together to build community, address collective needs, and work for the benefit of the public. Collectively these organizations have a broad scope of activities, touching almost every aspect of Canadian life (Statistics Canada 2004). The study also documented a number of challenges for these organizations in achieving their missions, particularly accessing or developing sufficient funding and having sufficient capacity to meet growing needs.

An estimated 161,000 non-profit and voluntary organizations, according to the findings, were operating in Canada in 2003. Included in this total was a wide diversity of organizations: daycare centres, sports clubs, arts organizations, social clubs, private schools, hospitals, food banks, environmental groups, trade associations, places of worship, advocates for social justice, and groups that raise funds to cure diseases. Their two common characteristics were the pursuit of goals to serve the public or their members and an institutional form not allowing profits to be distributed to owners or directors. The primary areas of activity were sports and recreation (21% of all organizations), religion (19%), social services (12%), grant-making, fundraising, and voluntarism promotion (10%), arts and culture (9%), and development and housing (8%). Among the categories included were hospitals, universities and colleges, law, advocacy and politics, environment, education and research, health, and international organizations.

Most non-profit and voluntary organizations provide products or services for people. They often have a local focus, concentrate on the needs of specific sectors of the population, and operate within their own neighbourhood, city, town, or rural municipality. While many serve the

---

2   All data cited on the NSNVO findings come directly from this report.

general public, others target their services to specific populations, such as children, youth, seniors, persons with disabilities, and immigrant and racialized communities.

The NSNVO study revealed important differences between organizations with respect to earning relatively large revenues versus gaining modest incomes, being dependent or not on government funding, and reliance mainly on volunteers or on paid staff to accomplish the organizational missions. Another difference of significance was that just over half the organizations were registered as charities, allowing exemption from a variety of taxes and enabling their donors to claim tax credits for donations made.

The study also documented the substantial economic presence of this sector. Total revenues reported were $112 billion. Although one-third of this could be attributed to a relatively small number of hospitals, universities and colleges, the remaining organizations still reported revenues of $75 billion. Non-profit and voluntary organizations as a whole were reported to employ just over two million paid staff.

Peter Elson and Peyton Carmichael (2022) note that the NSNVO findings show that when hospitals, colleges and universities are included in the non-profit and voluntary sector, Canada had the second largest non-profit workforce in the world as a share of the economically active population, accounting for 6.9% of the Canadian GDP (in 2004 figures). However, non-profit hospitals, colleges, and universities now account for so much more economic activity than the rest of the sector that they are routinely statistically separated so the overall picture of the sector is not distorted. Elson and Carmichael's observations correspond with the historically important distinction in interpreting statistics for the sector, between QUANGOs (quasi-non-government organizations such as hospitals, colleges, and universities, also referred to as the para-public sector) and the core non-profit sector.

State of the Sector Report Ontario

The SOSR research project was commissioned by the Ontario Ministry of Citizenship as one commitment in its Partnership Project (Government of Ontario 2013). It provides a profile of the core non-profit sector in Ontario, including registered charities, incorporated nonprofits, and unincorporated community organizations. The survey work excluded hospitals, colleges, and universities, as well as public and Catholic schools and boards and public libraries. Although specific to Ontario, the research provides an important relatively recent large-scale survey of the sector that can be compared with the results of the NSNVO and other studies.[3] The detailed nature of this survey in Canada's largest province makes it particularly useful for closer examination.

The research was carried out by Pollara Strategic Insights between October 2012 and February 2013. It employed a mixed methodology of telephone and online surveys for a total sample size of 3,567 respondents. To identify the target organizations, Pollara created an inventory with contact information and eliminated duplication from sources, including from T3010 Information Returns for registered charities, contact information provided by grant applicants to the Ontario Trillium Foundation, businesses with Standard Industry Classification codes indicating a non-profit sector operation, and a register of incorporated non-profit sector organizations provided by the Ontario Ministry of Government Services.

Respondents included more than 3,500 core voluntary organizations operating as a nonprofit (33%) and/or as a registered charity (65%) in Ontario. They represented a statistically significant sample (approximately 6.4%) of the more than 55,000 non-profit sector organizations registered in Ontario in terms of primary activities (or subsectors) as well as geographic distribution. Data was categorized to permit comparisons with the NSNVO and other similar surveys over time, and the classification of subsectors corresponds with International Classification of Non-profit Organizations recommended by the United Nations.

Key Findings

The research confirmed that the core non-profit sector is vital to Ontario, including over 55,000 organizations generating some $67 billion in revenues and serving multiple missions vital to communities. The research also revealed the diversity of the sector, ranging from large corporately structured charities to "kitchen-table" nonprofits. It found no such thing as a "typical" nonprofit; they have specialized missions and objectives. Their services and programs comprise a broad range of activities targeted to unique communities and groups of people, from

---

3   All data cited in this section are from the *State of the Sector* report. It is noteworthy that author Ted Richmond was employed by the Ontario Public Service at the time of this report and was directly involved in its creation and its oversight.

young to old and newcomers to locals. The rich range of programs and activities includes arts and culture, sport and recreation, social and settlement services, environmental protection, fundraising, and international development.

The findings revealed some significant trends, including the resilience of the core non-profit sector in Ontario. Securing sufficient funds to continue to meet organizational and operational goals was an ongoing concern for most organizations, with three-quarters of respondents finding it challenging to generate enough revenue to fulfill their missions and achieve their objectives, and two-thirds reporting difficulties in meeting day-to-day needs. Yet the data gathered showed the respondents' organizations were growing modestly during challenging economic times. Non-profit organizations were still struggling to recover from the so-called Great Recession of the 2009 global financial crisis. For two-thirds, revenue had increased or stayed the same over the three years 2009–12. Only two in five reported receiving government funding, and of these, more than half said it had been stable or increased over the period.

The core non-profit sector is enduring; most organizations surveyed in the Ontario survey had been operating for more than twenty years. On average, registered charities have been serving much longer than other nonprofits. The "youngest" organizations (by mean years of operation) were those focused on law, advocacy and politics and on international activities, with a midrange for years of operation of seven and five years respectively. Most organizations surveyed were incorporated: a third as nonprofits and two-thirds as registered charities (and 27% as both).

The overview findings also revealed significant disparities within the sector. Overall, nonprofits in Ontario reported an average of just over $1.3 million in revenues, for a total estimated sector contribution of nearly $67 billion. At the same time, nearly one in four organizations (23%) reported annual revenues of less than $25,000. International activities organizations had the highest average revenues, at just under $3.6 million, while those operating in the arts and culture field the lowest average, at just under $433,000.

For the majority of organizations responding to the survey, the primary service area was a neighbourhood (61%), indicating that they are truly community-based organizations. Six percent stated that they operated province-wide, and an equal proportion on a pan-Canadian basis. Nine in ten organizations said that they served people, while one in three stated that they served other organizations (categories not exclusive). The most commonly serviced groups were the general public (29%) and children/young people (23%). Thirteen percent of the organizations indicated that they served immigrants, visible minority populations or other specific cultures or ethnic groups. Among respondents, organizations that focused on social services (18%), sports and recreation (13%), and religion (20%) were the leading types of nonprofits in most regions across the province. But upwards of one in four participants reported activities other than their primary one — most often education, social services, and/or grant-making — with 25% of health organizations reporting activities in the social services sphere.

Service and stability were the top organizational goals reported (35% and 32% respectively). Service is the *raison d'être* of every nonprofit, and for most respondents, this means meeting community needs and expanding current programs to reach more people. Stability is an essential internal operational goal to provide service, and the leading impetus here was finding more revenue sources. The precarious funding base of many nonprofits is a constant challenge for organizations, especially those that are small- and medium-sized.

The two top goals identified in terms of government support were assistance with the funding process (44%) and capacity-building (37%). Capacity-building is an important issue in terms of positioning the organization to survive sudden shocks like the pandemic — to be resilient. Other important goals reported were relationship-building and promoting public awareness of sector value (31%) and facilitating partnerships with business (16%).

Compared to the NSNVO research for Ontario conducted in 2003, similar proportions of organizations operate at the local level (60%, down 5 points from 2003), while 20% of organizations operate in a region of a province (+2) and 6% operate provincially (no change). Development and housing (6% of all paid staff) and business associations (2% of all paid staff) showed the greatest shifts in share of paid staff from the 2003 NSNVO results; eight of thirteen subsectors showed marginal or no change in share of paid staff compared to the NSNVO. Compared to 2003, sports and recreation organizations have a proportionally lower share of volunteers (40% of volunteers in 2003, at 13% of all volunteers in 2012), and social services organizations represented a larger share of the volunteer corps (23%, up 16 points from 2003 to 2012).

New methods of revenue generation are available, but uptake is limited. Only 1% of responding organizations said that they collected funds from social financing, generating an average of $41,686 from this source. Less than 5% of organizations say that they generate revenues through social enterprise; those that do, raise an average of $130,566 this way. As in 2003, funding (revenues) remained the top-noted issue for nonprofits in Ontario and by all indications in other provinces as well. The prominence of funding issues for nonprofits is not surprising given the precarious nature of much of the financing of the sector.

More Recent Data from Statistics Canada

In 2019 Statistics Canada published partial but significant updates on the data from the NSNVO (2019b). The findings show a sector that is growing but also reveal that by 2017 the core non-profit sector was declining slightly, relative to government and business nonprofits. For these 2019 reports, Statistics Canada divides the overall non-profit sector into three broad categories. Community non-profit institutions are engaged in activities like social and health services, advocacy, and sports and recreation (corresponding roughly to the "core" non-profit sector) provided for free or for minimal cost. Government nonprofits include hospitals, some residential care facilities, universities, and colleges. They are independently constituted, registered charities, and formally separate from government. But they are also under substantial governmental regulation (hence, the term "para-public sector organizations" also used to describe them). Business nonprofits include organizations such as chambers of commerce, business associations, and condominium associations. They provide goods and services at prices that are economically significant, and they have limits on how they may redistribute any surplus.

When the non-profit sector was viewed separately from government nonprofits, business and professional associations including trade unions (20.3%) accounted for the largest share of the non-profit sector. This was followed by social services (17.5%) and culture and recreation (14.5%). Expressed by type of organization or activity and including all nonprofits, in 2017 the largest share of activities was associated with health (41.5%) and education (30.1%). The next largest portion was social services (9.9%), including child and family services (Statistics Canada 2019b).

As mentioned, according to the summary of the findings from the satellite accounts and surveys on volunteering (Statistics Canada 2019b), economic activity in the non-profit sector totaled $169.2 billion in 2017, representing 8.5% of Canada's GDP. The most significant portion of non-profit activity (73.2%) came from government non-profit institutions, such as hospitals and universities. Community non-profit institutions accounted for 16.4% of the overall sector, while business non-profit institutions accounted for 10.4%.

Other Organizations Linked to the Non-profit Sector

To gain a fuller understanding of the non-profit sector we need to consider the broad range of organizations that stretch beyond narrowly defined non-profit boundaries. Many such organizations are generally seen to be part of institutions that operate in the private marketplace but embody non-profit types of features that distinguish them from for-profit businesses and/or link them to the non-profit sector. These organizations and the spaces they occupy, consequently, constitute components of the political economy resting at the edges of the market and non-profit sectors. It is important to position these bodies within society to gain a more holistic understanding of the non-profit sector.

Cooperatives

Statistics Canada provided official statistics on cooperatives in Canada in the report *Co-operatives in Canada* (2019a), based on data from 2018. The data was for non-financial cooperatives that are corporations legally incorporated under specific federal, provincial, or territorial legislation and owned by an association of persons seeking to satisfy common needs, such as access to products or services, sale of products or services, or employment. The study did not include financial cooperatives, such as credit unions and caisses populaires, which are governed by separate legislation.

The 2018 data showed a small but constant growth in cooperatives in Canada in terms of their total numbers and their revenue. Using official Statistics Canada definitions (2019b), nearly two-thirds (63.2%) of the reported total of 5,846 active non-financial cooperatives were nonprofits. Quebec had the largest share of active cooperatives (44.4%), followed by Ontario (18.9%). In that year Canadian cooperatives generated $52.9 billion in total revenues, held $42.5 billion in total assets, employed 103,470 people, and paid $2.4 billion in salaries and wages. Two-thirds (66.6%) of these cooperatives were consumer cooperatives, 16.1% producer cooperatives, 9.4% multi-stakeholder, 6.6% worker cooperatives, and 1.3% federations.

More than half of active non-financial cooperatives operated in the real estate and rental and leasing industries (33.4%), in wholesale and retail trade (14.5%), and in health care and social assistance (8.7%). In that year 52.1% of cooperatives were run by unpaid employees and had no paid staff. Nearly all these organizations (99.1%) were small or medium-sized enterprises with fewer than 500 employees.

A special Senate report published by the Government of Canada in 2012 examined the status of cooperatives in Canada. It stated that cooperatives and credit unions are driven by both economic and social concerns and differ from individual businesses and corporations in the following three important ways:

- their main objectives are to meet the needs of their members rather than to maximize profits;
- control over co-operatives is exercised democratically by their members, who have equal power (one member, one vote), rather than being determined by the number of shares held in the business;
- the profits of co-operatives are redistributed to their members on the basis of how much they use the co-op, not the amount of capital they have invested. (Government of Canada 2012, 2)

The report also outlined the seven basic principles of the international cooperative movement:

1. voluntary and open membership,
2. democratic member control and equal voting rights,
3. member economic participation to the capital of their co-operative,
4. autonomy and independence to preserve the democratic power,
5. education, training,
6. cooperation among co-operatives locally, nationally and internationally,
7. concern for the sustainable development of the community (2–3)

The same report identified two main associations representing cooperatives in Canada. The Canadian Co-operative Association represents cooperatives operating in anglophone regions, while the Conseil canadien de la coopération et de la mutualité represents those in francophone areas. The mission of both associations is to promote the cooperative model, support the development of cooperatives, and represent cooperatives to government (3).

In their edited collection *Co-operative Canada*, Brett Fairbairn and Nora Russell (2014) report a total of about nine thousand cooperatives, including credit unions, in communities of all sizes across Canada — a number which continues to grow. These community-based enterprises have eighteen million members across Canada — more than half the population of the country. The editors also report an estimate by the International Co-operative Alliance (ICA) of about one billion members of cooperatives globally, generating more that 100 million jobs and employing close to a quarter of the world's population. These editors cite the ICA definition of a cooperative adopted by regional, national, and international networks of cooperatives:

> an autonomous association of persons united voluntarily to meet their common economic, social and cultural needs and aspirations through a jointly owned and democratically controlled enterprise. (9)

Fairbairn and Russell also highlight the elements of association, enterprise, and needs-based activities, and the qualifying terms autonomous, voluntary, joint, and democratic. These characteristics are fundamental to defining cooperatives, in their view, rather than the specific legal form of the enterprise.

Three important distinguishing features of cooperatives are outlined. The first is that they address specific needs of distinct groups of people, unlike general-purpose development organizations, such as community development corporations. Another is the exceptional commitment of cooperatives to democratic member control and member economic participation. The third element, according to Fairbairn and Russell, is that the general aim of all cooperatives is to meet the needs of their own members rather than outside groups — making their missions distinct from much of the remainder of the non-profit sector.

Fairbairn and Russell emphasize that cooperatives develop and augment reservoirs of social cohesion and social capital, providing communities with resources to deal with imperatives of change or opportunities for innovation. They are also unique in the degree to which their functioning depends on multiple active networks. An additional feature highlighted in *Co-operative Canada* is the role of cooperatives in community development (see also Gingras and Carrier 2014, 139–157; Ketilson 2014 209–233).

In an appendix on terminology for the non-profit sector, Fairbairn and Russell (2014, 254–272) describes the language of "community economic development" as covering similar terrain to that of the social economy in Quebec. Two organizations highlighted are the Canadian Community Economic Development Network and the Canadian Co-operative Association.

Social Enterprises

The *Canadian National Social Enterprise Sector Survey Report* (Elson, Hall, and Wamucii 2016)[4] was designed to map the location, purpose, and operations of social enterprises in Canadian provinces and territories (excluding Quebec, where separate research had been done). The researchers defined "social enterprise" as a business venture owned or operated by a non-profit organization selling goods or providing services in the market for the purpose of creating a blended return on investment, both financial and social/environmental/cultural. Data was aggregated from 1,350 social enterprises across Canada providing sufficiently complete responses, and financial averages were based on estimates from the 932 responding social enterprises which provided complete financial data. The research found that the responding organizations had a variety of purposes (multiple responses allowed):

- 26% for employment development
- 19% for workforce integration
- 19% to generate income for a parent organization
- 81% to achieve a social mission
- 45% carry out a cultural mission
- 27% have an environmental mission
- 43% address poverty reduction.

---

4   All references in this section are to Elson, Hall and Wamucii (2016).

On average, the responding social enterprises had 200 individual members and 13 organizational members, totalling to at least 254,000 individual members and 17,000 organizational memberships. The sector appears to be relatively mature, with organizations reporting a median age of twenty-two years.

Social enterprises provided paid employment for at least 31,000 full-time, part-time, seasonal, and contract workers, earning over $442 million in wages and salaries. Leaving out contract workers, the labour force in these enterprises is an estimated 15,000 full-time equivalent employees. At least 23,000 people were employed as part of the mission of the social enterprise, such as persons with disabilities and/or other employment barriers. The survey also documented the involvement of at least 116,000 full- and part-time volunteers.

These organizations provided services to over 5.5 million people; at least 116,000 of these received training for workforce integration. Of the total revenue of $1.2 billion reported for 2013–14, the sales of goods and services was at least $828 million or nearly 70% of revenue. Social enterprises in Canada average $1.1 million in total revenues, with $846,000 in sales. The responding organizations had an average of $62,000 in net profit/surplus.

Nearly three-quarters of social enterprises received government grants from the three levels of government in Canada: provincial funding was the largest, followed by federal, and then municipal. Other sources, also in declining order, were private individuals, foundations, and corporations. Twenty-three percent of social enterprises in Canada received no grants. Some social enterprises had used loans of various kinds, but nearly three-quarters received no loans.

Like co-operatives, social enterprises and their staff are highly networked. The same individual may have multiple, intersecting connections to a social enterprise, as member, recipient of training, employment and services, employee or volunteer.

The Social Economy in Quebec

The term social economy has evolved to have a distinct meaning in Quebec society, broader than both social enterprise and nonprofit as commonly understood in the rest of Canada. In an appendix to Fairbairn and Russell (2014, 261), Fairbairn notes that the notion of the "social economy" developed in Europe in the 1970s and spread to Canada, particularly Quebec, where the économie sociale is well established and provides a focus for research and public policy. In 1996 the Quebec government organized a socio-economic summit from which grassroots and community groups organized a task force on the social economy, leading to the formal establishment of the Chantier de l'économie sociale as an autonomous association in 1999. The Chantier plays a prominent role in Quebec's social economy, along with the federation of Quebec's cooperatives, the Conseil Québécois de la cooperation et de la mutualité.

Statistics from the Chantier describe Quebec's social economy as comprising over 11,200 collective enterprises with overall sales exceeding $47.8 billion, or more than the construction, aeronautic, and mining industries combined. Over 220,000 people work in the social economy every day, in all sectors of activity from retail to the emerging technologies (Chantier de l'économie sociale 2020).

As noted by Fairbairn and Russell (2014, 262), organizations are considered part of *l'économie sociale* based principally on their role in society, rather than their legal form. The Chantier defines the social economy as an economic sector composed of associations representing solidarity, autonomy, and citizenship. These values are expressed through the five principles of community service, autonomous management, democratic decision-making, placing people and work before capital and profits, and participation, empowerment, and individual or collective accountability.

Marguerite Mendell and Nancy Neamtan (2010) report that the social economy continues to develop as an integral part of the political economy of Quebec, but as in Canada and internationally, there is not adequate data to reflect this. Because of these gaps in the data, their paper "The Social Economy in Quebec: Towards a New Political Economy" used 2002 Quebec government data from the Bureau de l'économie sociale and the Direction des cooperatives. The data, while incomplete, allows us to sketch a rough picture of the size of the Quebec social economy.

Mendell and Neamtan (2010) found that the Quebec government data (from 2002) showed that the social economy in Quebec included 7,822 businesses (3,881 co-operatives and 3,941 non-profit organizations), including 935 childcare centers, 671 credit unions, 180 worker cooperatives, 103 social economy enterprises providing help to households, and 72 shareholding workers cooperatives. The latter consists of businesses in which the employees have acquired shares. Worker-shareholder cooperatives are a form of cooperatives specific to Quebec (Innovation, Science and Economic Development Canada 2018, 3).

These enterprises, not including credit unions, had total annual sales of $17.2 billion, of which $15.9 billion was for cooperatives and $1.3 billion for nonprofits. If credit unions are included, the total sales for cooperatives rises to $101.2 billion. Still not including credit unions, they created 124,302 jobs, 79,222 in cooperatives and 45,080 in nonprofits. With credit unions included the job creation total for cooperatives rises to 116,222.

Philanthropic Foundations

Philanthropic foundations play a unique role in the non-profit ecosystem in Canada. Because their grants are sourced from the foundations' own assets, they can reflect priorities and needs that differ from the dominant orientation of government funders at all levels, with their preference for short-term contracts for services matching their current political priorities. Furthermore, foundations have the option of subsidizing the type of community research and advocacy that has been virtually eliminated from government portfolios. Canadian foundations therefore represent a modest but important counterbalance to the weight of the neoliberal funding regime and the corresponding loss of autonomy for community organizations. Of course, it should be noted here that there are also some neoliberal-oriented foundations, whose mission is in support of broader neoliberal change.

Philanthropic Foundations Canada (PFC) is a member association of Canadian grantmakers, including private and public foundations, charities, and corporations. The PFC provides support to its members and organized philanthropy through public policy work, building awareness of philanthropic contributions, and providing shared learning opportunities for funders (PFC 2021). In "Canadian Foundation Facts" (PFC 2021), the organization identifies private and public foundations as two types of registered charities in Canada, along with charitable organizations. Canadian foundations are described as a diverse group of funders, dispersed across the country, that contribute close to $6 billion annually to qualified donees. Private foundations are controlled by a single donor or family through a board made up of a majority of directors who are not at arm's length. A public (or community) foundation, in contrast, is governed by a board that is made up of a majority of directors at arm's length. A private foundation is not allowed to engage in any business activity, but it can operate its own charitable program.

Community foundations build up an endowment to serve a particular geographic community. Donors can set up individual funds in a community foundation and have as little or as much control as they wish in deciding on disbursements from those funds. Donors can also choose to contribute funds to the community foundation's general endowment fund, leaving the board of directors to distribute the income from this fund according to needs and opportunities in the community.

In March 2021, reports the PFC, there were 86,527 charities in Canada, of which 4,961 were public foundations and 6,189 private foundations.[5] The proportion of foundations to charities remained relatively stable, about 12% of registered charities. In 2018 public and private foundations had about $91.9 billion in assets, with nearly 39% held by community foundations and the remaining 61% by private foundations.[6] Total grants were about $7 billion, with community foundations providing nearly double the amount as private. Many public foundations are attached to institutions like hospitals, which distribute larger portions of their funds annually.

In *Assets and Giving Trends of Canada's Grantmaking Foundations*, Imagine Canada and Philanthropic Foundations of Canada (2014) profile the assets and giving trends of Canada's 150 largest grantmaking foundations and ten largest community foundations over a ten-year period from 2002 to 2012. They report that this support is distributed widely. In 2011, the vast majority made grants to qualified donees working in the areas of education and research (86%), health (78%), and social services (78%). Over half contributed to the areas of arts and culture (59%), international (57%), and religion (57%). Less than half gave to the areas of development and housing (45%), grantmaking and voluntarism (41%), sports and recreation (39%), and law, advocacy, and politics (36%). The lowest portion of foundations made grants to environment organizations (28%) or to some level of government (15%).

In 2017, the PFC and Community Foundations of Canada (CFC) published the results of a survey designed to better understand

---

5 Source: Canada Revenue Agency (list of charities, online data as of March 2021).
6 Source: Lasby, 2021. The assets of private foundations include Mastercard Foundation, with $23.7 billion in assets.

philanthropic foundations in Canada. It was carried out as part of a global research effort to develop comparative data and information on institutional philanthropy around the world, led by researchers at the Harvard Kennedy School at Harvard University. The research report, *A Portrait of Canadian Foundation Philanthropy*, identified important trends from the fifty-four organizations responding to the survey. One such trend was steady growth of the private foundation sector in Canada, with more families and donors interested in committing to institutional philanthropy. Another trend, new for Canada, was a larger number of very big private foundations with assets over the billion-dollar mark. Imagine Canada and PFC (2014) states as well that of the six very large foundations (i.e., with assets over $100 million in 2012) created since 2002, five are based in Ontario — including the two largest: MasterCard Foundation and Li Ka Shing (Canada) Foundation.

Other developments noted in *A Portrait of Canadian Foundation Philanthropy* were a growing influence of younger "millennial" leaders in the sector, an increase in the number of organized funder affinity groups focused on specific issues, such as Indigenous philanthropy, mental health, youth, and homelessness, and a greater commitment to developing shared practices with respect to systemic policy issues such as climate change, sustainable development, urbanization, reconciliation with Indigenous populations, and integration of migrants and refugees (PFC 2017).

Putting the Pieces Together

Service and advocacy, as previously noted, are the two key functions played by nonprofits in Canadian society. Research consistently shows the key role of the sector in providing a host of supports to the general public, particularly to vulnerable populations with limited access to services provided by the private and state sectors. The advocacy role is also a vital form of service, promoting civic engagement and giving a voice to the communities they serve.

Canada has one of the largest and most vibrant non-profit and voluntary sectors in the world. It encompasses "service delivery" organizations in areas such as health, education, social services, community development, and housing, as well as those that provide "expressive" functions in arts and culture, religion, sports, recreation, civic advocacy, environmental protection, and through business, labour, and professional associations (Hall et al. 2005). The data suggests that the non-profit sector is not just filling gaps in state provision but is also taking over core policy domains in realms such as affordable housing, immigration settlement services, and home care support for the elderly. Its public role is growing, to address both increasing social diversity and growing public sector costs.

The official data clearly show that the non-profit sector in Canada has not only been growing in size but is also becoming more divided between organizations with relatively large revenues and staff, and those with substantially less. It is clear as well that the official numbers may significantly underestimate the size of the sector. One of the main reasons for this was reported as follows by a Statistics Canada spokesperson:

> Obtaining reliable data on the number of NPOs is no easy task: The greatest number of those non-profit organizations exist in the form of a voluntary association, meaning they are not incorporated. If they are not incorporated, it's even less likely that we count them. (Special Senate Committee on the Charitable Sector 2019, 114)

But other factors as well may lead to an important underestimation of the number of non-profit organizations in Canada. The cooperative movement, for example, considers all its member organizations to be part of the non-profit sector (Fairbairn and Russell 2014), yet for purposes related to different legal statuses of cooperatives, Statistics Canada only classifies about two-thirds of them as such (Statistics Canada 2019a). Similarly, the organizations, policy makers, and academics associated with the social economy in Quebec count their constituent organizations on the basis of social mission rather than formal legal classification.[7]

When the diverse landscape of the non-profit sector in Canada is examined, researchers and policy advocates too often find only what they are searching for. Trade unions, for example, have played a giant role in the struggles for economic and social rights in Canada for more than a century. Yet, although Statistics Canada classifies them as nonprofits (Statistics Canada 2019b), they are rarely mentioned in that context. Also largely overlooked in the field of non-profit social services

---

7   Note that the institutional definition of the social economy in Quebec does not include private foundations, hospitals, colleges, university, or churches.

are Indigenous social service providers working in and outside of urban environments. Another oft-neglected reality is that non-Christian faith organizations play a significant role, often undocumented, in bringing essential social services to their congregations, including refugees and recent immigrants. Community legal clinics in Ontario, although completely funded by the Ontario government through Legal Aid Ontario, are run by community boards, a practice that has provided sufficient autonomy to maintain an active tradition of advocacy for the social, economic, and legal rights of lower-income citizens. These are just some of the many examples showing that the non-profit sector is considerably larger than commonly depicted.

Until recently, the non-profit sector, both in Canada and internationally, was invisible and largely ignored. Only in the last two decades has it come to be understood and defined as a distinct sector (Laforest 2011b). The trend has been to define the sector negatively, for what it is not — neither for-profit nor government. But it should be portrayed in terms of its positive features: mission-driven, providing vital services, and building community engagement, often with a social justice orientation.

From an increased awareness of the sector as distinct has arisen a range of new names for it, some of which are far from satisfactory. As mentioned in Chapter 1, the generic term "charitable" ignores the tens of thousands of non-profit organizations that are not registered charities, while describing the sector as "voluntary" captures some of the spirit of the sector but deflects from the harsh reality that nonprofits cannot provide their services without adequate funding. Combining these two terms to create the "voluntary and charitable sector" further muddies the waters.

We, as well as many researchers and scholars in the field, therefore continue to name the sector as "non-profit" or perhaps "voluntary and non-profit" (Elson 2009 and 2016; Fairbairn and Russell 2014; Liao 2017; Mulé and Desantis 2017; Joy and Shields 2020). At the same time, some nonprofits and academics are starting to refer to the "public benefit sector" to emphasize that all the activities of the sector, including advocacy, are of benefit to Canadians as a whole:

> It means bringing alive the mission and mandate of "for public good" organizations and agencies. It means acknowledging that anti-racism — anti-Indigenous and anti-Black racisms are "public goods." (Douglas 2020a)

Terminology for the non-profit sector and its various sub-sectors is therefore inconsistent and continuing to evolve. And better data on the sector, more frequently published, is a vital need. No single source of statistics provides a full picture of the sector as a whole.

It is essential, therefore, to consider the sector through both the "macro" and the "micro" lenses to take full account of its size, its economic impact, and the range of its activities. When we focus on particular types of non-profit organizations, such as cooperatives or social enterprises, community service organizations or private foundations, we can lose sight of the dynamics of the sector as a whole. When we try to present a portrait of the entire sector, however, we may obscure important or unique features of one or more of its constituent parts. Nevertheless, a "big picture" analysis remains essential for policy development. A holistic approach is also crucial for public education concerning the vital role of the non-profit sector in the Canadian economy, in health and social services, and in advocacy for domestic and global equity and human rights.

CHAPTER 3

Financial and Human Resources in the Non-profit Sector

Understanding the financial and human resources of the non-profit sector is essential for a critical consideration of the place of non-profits in Canadian society. How the non-profit sector is funded, and the structures of its financial architecture, can tell us much about the nature of the sector. The impacts on nonprofits of neoliberal restructuring have been considerable. The role of competitive contract financing of non-profit delivery of public services, for example, has been significant, with many negative consequences for the non-profit sector and communities served. Non-profit organizations have come to be more dependent on short-term, strings-attached financing, often altering the missions of organizations and forcing the adoption of leaner and more business-oriented operating structures (Joy and Shields 2020). Neoliberal approaches have also squeezed non-profit organizations to absorb more of the costs for delivering public services, resulting in growing mismatches between public needs and demands for services and the ability of the non-profit sector to meet this demand. The resulting "social deficit" in unmet need is expected to rapidly expand to $25 billion by 2026 (Imagine Canada 2018b). The impact of the COVID-19 pandemic and inflationary economic disruptions in the wake of the pandemic have widened societal polarization and inevitably deepened the social deficit further.

Nonprofits need financial resources for their activities — mainly to pay staff, including staff who train and supervise volunteers, and for administration and community activities, including outreach and needs assessment, education, and advocacy. Carrying out these activities are the "human resources," both paid staff and volunteers.

For non-profit organizations not run solely by volunteers, wages plus benefits for staff at different levels and positions are the biggest single cost. Volunteers of different types, including unpaid interns, are the other essential component of "human resources" — for many nonprofits, they are the sole form.

The funding for these resources includes grants and contributions from all three levels of government, revenue-generating activities of various kinds, and grants from different types of foundations. Donations from individuals are also part of their revenues; for some organizations they represent a major source of revenue. Social finance initiatives have also arisen as new, "innovative" funding sources.

The trends in both financial and human resources for the non-profit sector are of course tightly intertwined. Analyzing these patterns provides a good lens for understanding the evolution of the sector and the stresses and tensions within it. In particular, as noted, for non-profit organizations that provide public services through contracts, the impact of neoliberal restructuring on nonprofit–state relationships has been profound.

A Vital Part of the Canadian Economy

As noted in Chapter 2 in relation to the scale and scope of the non-profit sector, there are greater than 170,000 incorporated non-profit organizations and many times this number of smaller, less formally constituted, locally based voluntary bodies in operation in Canada. The non-profit sector's contribution to the Canadian economy is substantive, representing close to a tenth of the country's GDP, with the core non-profit sector standing at 4% of GDP (Imagine Canada n.d.). These figures only capture the economic activities of the formal components of the non-profit sector, with the nonincorporated and voluntary activities of the larger non-profit sector not covered in such statistics. The sector's economic impact is, consequently, more pronounced than market-based criteria suggest.

General Non-profit Financial Resources

Additional details regarding the financial dimensions of the broader non-profit sector are found in Chapter 2, but the essential dimensions include the following statistics. Data from 2019 indicates that registered charities alone — only a portion of Canada's nonprofits — received a total of about $260 billion in income. Grants and contributions from government represented the largest share of revenue for the sector (+/- $199 billion). Earned and investment income combined was second, at +/- $36 billion, while fundraising represented at +/- $26 billion (Government of Canada 2021a).

Data from 2017 (Statistics Canada 2019b[1]) shows that, when measured by type of organization, the bulk of non-profit activity was in health (41.5%) and education (30.1%). Next came services (9.9%), including child and family services. When activity is considered without the para-public sector, business and professional associations, including trade unions, accounted for the largest single portion, at 20.3%. This was followed by social services (17.5%) and culture and recreation (14.5%).

Looking at income sources and types of organizations, core sector nonprofits received nearly a third of their income from governments. Another 27.8% came from sales, and 17.8% from donations by individuals and households. Membership fees were 14.1%, while investment income combined with donations from businesses and other sources totalled less than 6%.

In the para-public sector, most of the income (72.9%) came from government sources, mainly provincial. The sale of goods and services represented 21.3% of income, while investment income, donations, and transfers from business and other institutions each represented less than 3% of the total.

Business nonprofits and non-profit institutions serving households, include organizations such as chambers of commerce, business associations, and condominium associations. More than three-fifths of 2017 income (61.6%) was generated by the sale of goods and services, membership fees (such as condominium association fees) were 33.8% of total income, and other sources were less than 5%.

Donations as a Source of Funding

Non-profit organizations are vehicles for citizen engagement as well as providers of essential health and social services and recreational activities. Individual Canadians support nonprofits and shape their priorities through direct donations and by taking out individual memberships

---

1 Data in the following paragraphs are from Statistics Canada (2019b).

— $8 billion and $139 million respectively in 2002–03, according to the NSNVO (Statistics Canada 2004). These contributions allow individuals to contribute to the well-being of their fellow citizens or advance principles and values in which they believe (Statistics Canada 2012). Governments in Canada recognize these contributions by providing income tax credits as a portion of individual donations made to registered charities — this represents a form of government tax expenditure supporting non-profit activities, as well as a vehicle of citizen engagement.

While the mix of funding from governments, corporations, foundations, and revenue-generating activities varies considerably from one organization to another, donations represent an important source of revenue for many nonprofits. This is true not only for nonprofits in the core sector, but also for larger charities that can be considered as para-public or QUANGOs, such as hospitals and education organizations that solicit donations through affiliated or non-affiliated foundations as well as individual private donors.

Data from Imagine Canada (2018a) showed that more than $14 billion was donated to registered charities in 2014. Over a quarter of these funds went to four areas of activity: religion, health, social services, and international organizations. As well, most Canadians expressed confidence in charities, with four of five having some or a lot of trust in them. To facilitate the administrative work associated with donations, the organization CanadaHelps provides Canadian charities, large as well as small, with advanced technology for soliciting funds and processing donations (CanadaHelps 2021a).

The *Charitable Giving by Canadians* report (Statistics Canada 2012) provided details on donations to nonprofits for the years 2007 and 2010. Respondents were asked to report the amount of money they had given to charitable and non-profit organizations and which ones they were. This included donations that were tax-creditable (given to registered charities) as well as ones that were not. Of the $10.6 billion reported donations for 2010, the average annual amount per donor was $446 and the median amount was $123. Although women gave a bit more often than men, the average amount donated was basically equal for both men and women. Earlier research reviewed for the study showed that amounts of giving were higher for the employed, those with university degrees, and persons in higher-income households. Higher average annual donations were also associated with older persons, active participation in an organized religion, and volunteer engagement.

Some reasons for individuals giving more than others are altruistic: awareness of the needs, believing that the donation will make a difference, and the strength of pro-social values. Other reasons relate to perceived individual benefits, such as psychological well-being and self-esteem, tax advantages, social status, and reputation (Angelou 2022; CanadaHelps 2021c). The relative cost of the donation as a proportion of disposable income is a factor, as is the fact of being solicited and the way this is done.

In *The Giving Report 2021*,[2] CanadaHelps (2021b) outlined some significant recent trends in donations by individual Canadians to nonprofits. A continuing decline in the overall amount of donations is a cause for concern for organizations dependent on donations, but important positive trends were observed as well. In 2020, online giving accelerated at record rates — partly as a response to the COVID-19 crisis. Furthermore, donations to social service and Indigenous charities were at above average levels. An earlier report, *Canada Giving 2019* (CAF Canada 2019), identified an end to the gradual decline in international giving, with a marked increase for disaster relief. Data presented for the report on the non-profit sector by the Senate (Special Senate Committee on the Charitable Sector 2019) suggests that while total donations are increasing in Canada — during the initial phases of the pandemic starting in 2020 there was a large drop in donations (Draaisma 2022) — the number of donors is declining, and the proportion of seniors among these donors is steadily increasing. The decline in the number of donors and declines in volunteering have been referred to as a "social recession" (Elgenius 2018, 46), suggesting falling levels in community connectedness.

Another significant trend is the growing number of very large donations going to para-public institutions like hospitals and universities. Joe Friesen (2021), writing for the *Globe and Mail,* reports that between 2011 and 2018, the University of Toronto raised $2.6 billion through fundraising, including one donation of $100 million and another of $250 million. Friesen noted that university fundraising (and the same could be said for other para-public institutions like hospitals) has taken on added urgency as provincial government funding stagnates.

---

2   Report was prepared in collaboration with Imagine Canada using data from the Canada Revenue Agency.

Neoliberal governments, as part of offloading and shrinking the state, have called upon individual donations and corporate philanthropy to fill funding gaps. Many charitable organizations have deployed fundraising resources in an attempt to capture donations, especially from wealthy individuals and corporations. But it is the largest charities that have the capacity to successfully employ such resources and fundraising strategies. The result is an increasingly distorted pattern of giving, with a few large and well-positioned charities seeing increased levels of donations but the vast majority of charities (those of medium and small size) showing an ever-declining donation base. Also, for the wealthy and corporations, donations can have large tax advantages, representing a loss of tax revenue for governments, which can place strains on state finances.

Given that newcomers make up a constantly growing proportion of the Canadian population, especially in major cities such as Toronto, Vancouver, and Montréal, their patterns of donations to charities play an increasingly significant role. Derrick Thomas (2012) reported data showing that in 2010, immigrants were about as likely to donate money as were people born in Canada. The average and median amounts, however, were higher than those for the Canadian-born ($554 versus $409 and $155 versus $111, respectively). One reason behind these trends, according to Thomas, may be the higher level of religious affiliation and attendance for newcomers, as this factor is generally associated with higher levels of average individual donations. We should note as well that both donations and volunteer activities among newcomers, especially more recent immigrants, may be under-reported for a variety of reasons, including language factors that limit participation in surveys and various forms of support to their immediate community of time, or of in-kind or monetary donations, that go unreported.

A survey of more than 3,000 Canadians was conducted in 2020 by Imagine Canada, Ethnicity Matters, and a coalition of charities and nonprofits (Imagine Canada and Ethnicity Matters 2020). The study concluded that the communities surveyed — South Asian, Chinese, Filipino, Black (Afro-Caribbean/African), Arab, and Iranian — shared a strong willingness to embrace community service. It also found that newcomers to Canada and second-generation citizens are driven to give and volunteer out of a sense of duty to advance the well-being of their communities and Canadian society generally, with empathy for those in need deeply rooted in strong family and religious values.

Donations will continue to be an important source of revenue for the non-profit sector. Changing trends in giving do, however, pose challenges. The competition for such funds is increasing, and there is an increasing preponderance of donations to bigger charities, which poses a threat to the revenue base of smaller, more community-based nonprofits.

Social Finance and Social Impact Bonds

There is nothing very new about charities and other nonprofits acquiring additional revenue through earned income (see the discussion of social enterprises in Chapter 2). These initiatives include a wide range of activities which have come to be described by many as "social finance," in spite of the ambiguity of the term.[3] In Quebec, as in Western Europe, enterprises with a social purpose, including both non-profit and some for-profit, are categorized as part of the "social economy" (see the discussion of the social economy in Quebec in Chapter 2). But they are generally a distinct form of community-based financing of "businesses" for mutual benefit, like cooperatives and credit unions. In the rest of Canada, the term "social finance," more recently has become the general descriptor for the generation of private capital for public benefit and non-profit activities outside of government or foundation contracts and grants. Increasingly, social finance is viewed by many as the main or even the only way to bridge the gap between revenues and service demand in the non-profit sector. Senator Ratna Omidvar (2020) argues that, especially in the context where the only source of non-profit sector finance that has the potential to grow is earned revenue, government should reform tax law to allow nonprofits greater scope to engage in business ventures. One of the promises of social finance is that it can liberate privately held capital toward social purposes.

Social finance came to prominence with the rise of neoliberal austerity initiatives and has been part of the move to shift fiscal responsibility away from state support for public benefit programing (Pawelski 2015). Social finance is part of the larger financialization drive promoted by neoliberal economic logic that was behind the financial crisis of 2008–09. The logic behind social finance is to align private interest and private capital with social policy, with the assertion that private profit-making can be made compatible with the pursuit of public interests for support

---

3 See Fairbairn 2014 and Liao 2017 "The Changing Face of the Non-profit Sector: Social Enterprise Legislation in British Columbia," also in Fairbairn.

of public policy. In short, the contention is that private interests can do well by investing in "doing good" works (Harvie et al. 2021).

Social Impact Bonds

One prime instrument of social finance that has been cast as a creative way to help bridge the gap between client needs and sector revenues is the social impact bond (SIB). Writing in 2014, Andrew Galley, Elizabeth McIsaac, and Jamie Van Ymeren described SIBs as a new funding tool that uses private capital to fund preventative social interventions. More specifically, the SIB is intended to focus on impact and outcomes, with the potential of responding to challenging social policy problems and providing long-term savings for government. The interest in Canada for SIBs, which Galley, McIsaac, and Van Ymeren report as growing quickly, comes both from a move towards outcomes-based funding and programming and a growing interest in social finance. In Canada, the first SIB was announced in Saskatchewan in May 2014 — Sweet Dreams, a $1 million program designed to provide supportive housing for at-risk single mothers and their children. With this SIB, the expectation is that the mothers are supported with subsidized housing so that they can engage in education and training, and in some cases treatment programs, "empowering" the mothers to gain employment and allowing them to be in a position to keep their children out of the protective care system. Success is judged by how many children remain out of the child welfare system (Piller 2019). The saving for government from such outcomes can be substantive.

Nevertheless, Galley, McIsaac, and Van Ymeren identify important questions and potential controversy with this new funding model. Is it just a new way to describe government offloading of social spending? Will better outcomes and cost savings actually be realized? And what do SIBs mean for funding to the non-profit sector as a whole?

Jesse Hajer (2019) reported on the Province of Manitoba's first SIB project, Restoring the Sacred Bond, delivered in partnership with the Southern First Nations Network of Care. The two-year project was designed to target two hundred Indigenous mothers identified as at-risk of having their newborns taken into care by child welfare authorities. This SIB is designed along similar dimensions to Sweet Dreams. Hajer identifies SIBs as a form of partial privatization, where private investors finance social programs until they meet targeted objectives.

If the SIB hits its targets, investors are repaid by government at some predetermined rate of return. Since being introduced, SIBs have been controversial, Hajer reports, due to higher costs and payments to private investors. SIBs raised questions among both academics and community stakeholders as to whether private investors should be profiting from these projects, what the full impacts on vulnerable clients are, and what benefit government is getting from their payments to private investors.

Up front, SIBs are also more expensive, due to the complex agreements and negotiations involved, often requiring the hiring of specialist external expertise. This means that proportionally more money goes to lawyers and consultants and less to frontline service delivery. The higher costs under a SIB are often justified by the fact that government transfers risk to the private sector and only pays when targets are achieved. SIBs are also claimed to support innovative experimental projects that may be deemed too risky for government to fund directly. Neoliberal governments also argue that governments are too bureaucratic, lack innovative capacity, and are risk averse. SIBs, by contrast, allow government to tap into the innovative energies of the marketplace (Joy and Shields 2018). However, according to Hajer (2019), neither of these claims regarding risk appears to be holding up in practice. SIBs generally use program interventions with a demonstrated track record of success, often based on earlier public investment — which can discourage investments with the most vulnerable population groups due to the increased risks to investors of not reaching their target outcomes.

One example of the concerns of some academics about the politics of social impact bonds is that of Meghan Joy and John Shields (2018), who argue that SIBs are being used to privatize social policy, de-publicize social services, and turn individual vulnerability into a new form of profit making — all with negative consequences for democracy and social equity. SIBs focus on behaviour modification of vulnerable populations centred on such things as promotion of the work ethic, skills development, parental skills, health and nutrition education, mental toughness building, and such. Social problems come to be individualized, and the social determinants of need and vulnerability approach to understanding the complexity of social problems is ignored. Private investors in SIBs are to be rewarded for their success in transforming marginalized populations into good citizens who are not a drain on public finances (Joy and Shields 2016). There is also the implicit threat that those individuals who do not transform along acceptable paths will face sanctions. This promotes the development of a political narrative contrasting so-called "good citizens" with underserving dependent clients (Elgenius 2018, 54).

Despite these problems with a profit-making model of SIBs, approaches that embrace more community-centred orientations with the support of community and government financing hold some promise. Such an approach to SIBs is better able to place emphasis on tackling the roots of complex social problems with the involvement of nonprofits and citizens, opening up dialogue and experimentation concerning systemic roots of problems and solutions. One such innovation is an Indigenous-led investment group developing a SIB to tackle diabetes in Indigenous communities. Jeffrey Cyr, managing partner with the Vancouver-based firm Raven Indigenous Capital Partners, says that the proposed five-year bonds would reduce diabetes rates and medical expenses and provide community benefits such as improved access to healthy food (Stueck 2021), with the federal government paying returns of 5–9% to investors based on savings in health costs. Raven Indigenous Capital Partners is Canada's first Indigenous venture-capital intermediary, founded in 2018 by Jeff Cyr and two partners. Raven's objective is to transform historical power dynamics from dependency to self-determination, by letting communities set their own development priorities, collectively brainstorm solutions rooted in Indigenous values and knowledge, and connect with impact investors as well as foundations and government. The roots of this initiative go back to an Indigenous innovation summit supported by a variety of organizations, including the McConnell Foundation (Tiwari 2021). While Indigenous private capital is involved in this SIB, it is a business venture that departs from neoliberal financial logic and is rooted in the Indigenous community, embracing social goals.

Federal Support for Social Finance

For several decades, the federal government has confronted the tensions between maintaining essential health and social programs and reducing the funding for the non-profit organizations that deliver these services. The fiscal measures and tax policies of the Liberal government announced in 1995 by Liberal finance minister Paul Martin included both radical cutbacks in funding for nonprofits and changes to charity regulation designed to increase donations to many of these same organizations (Elson 2011, 101–109). In 2013, Conservative human resources minister Diane Finley outlined a plan detailing fifteen projects deemed promising candidates for social finance.

In 2018, the Fall Economic Statement of the Liberal government announced funding for a social finance fund intended to provide over $750 million over the following ten years.[4] Implementation was delayed due to the COVID-19 pandemic, but the 2021 federal budget recommitted to the launch of the program, with $220 million for first two years (Government of Canada 2021b).

According to Economic and Social Development Canada, the Social Finance Fund (SFF) seeks to accelerate the growth of Canada's social finance market and support charities, nonprofits, social enterprises, cooperatives, and other social purpose organizations in accessing flexible financing opportunities. Different portions of the fund will be allocated to particular communities on the basis of equity and inclusion. The SFF will provide repayable funds to a small number of "wholesalers," which will invest in existing or emerging social finance intermediaries, such as credit unions, community loan funds, and private equity firms with the goal of leveraging two dollars in private capital for each dollar of federal support (Government of Canada 2021b).

In keeping with the growing attention to social finance, various studies have been commissioned to examine not only the potential for social finance but also the practical obstacles to implementation for nonprofits. For example, the assessment commissioned by Immigration, Refugees and Citizenship Canada (IRCC 2016) found that the approach was favourable for dealing with longer-term needs, such as employment and social integration, but could not succeed without substantial government investment. Another report, *Are Charities Ready for Social Finance?* (Imagine Canada 2020a), drew on a survey of over a thousand Canadian charities to provide a comprehensive examination of the challenges, barriers, and potential opportunities that charities face when presented with social finance capital. The main challenges and barriers identified and addressed in the report included the small size of most Canadian charities; their lack of knowledge, experience, and expertise in social finance; and their risk aversion (particularly by boards of directors).

---

4   If we divide the total of the fund over its projected ten-year life span and assume that the project is successful in raising two more dollars for every dollar of initial funding, then this funding would be equal to about .085% of the annual revenues for the Canadian non-profit sector.

The more fundamental problem with neoliberal-based social finance, as outlined in the case of SIBs, is identified by David Harvie, Geoff Lightfoot, Simon Lilley, and Kenneth Weir (2021, 43):

> What appears as innovative in [social finance] is not a route to developing sustainable and responsible finance. Instead ... it represents an increased presence of capitalist imperatives pressing on the delivery of public services and social care projects.... [Social finance] ... works to promote the power of capital to determine the distribution of wealth. Hence we understand social investment as the most recent extension of neoliberal finance, where the apparatus of investment enables the logics of finance to deeper penetrate modes of social organizing, the provision of social care and the active depoliticization of the state.

Consequently, social finance, aside from some truly community-based versions of this approach, or funds directed to the social economy comprised of co-ops and credit unions, does not offer a desirable pathway for funding nonprofits and social policy more generally.

Human Resources

The Greatest Strength of the Non-profit Sector

The engine driving the non-profit sector is its human capital, as is noted regarding human resources in testimony to the Senate of Canada hearings on the non-profit sector:

> I have been asked to address the area of employment in the non-profit sector in Canada. This is an important dimension of the sector. If we consider employment as a measure of the size of the non-profit sector in Canada, Canada ranks second in the world with only the Netherlands outdistancing it. The sector as a whole employs about 2 million people and engages some 18 million volunteers. The non-profit service sector is human resource intensive. Indeed, human capital is viewed as being its greatest strength. Consequently, the state and well-being of the non-profit workforce is critical to the continued positive contribution of the sector to the economy and society. The sector as a whole contributes about 8.5 per cent

to the GDP. The core non-profit sector contributes something in the order of about 2.5 to 3 per cent of the GDP. The sector's work is highly gendered. About 70 to 80 per cent of the work is done by women. Caring work is typically associated with flexible work such as part-time employment. This highly gendered nature of the work, unfortunately, also reinforces the undervalued nature of non-profit employment. (Shields 2019)

Data on Employment and Compensation

Data from the satellite accounts of Non-profit Institutions and Volunteering show that average compensation per job was $57,000 in the non-profit sector in 2017. Employees in the government non-profit subsector (para-public organizations, or QUANGOs) received approximately $63,000, followed by employees in the business ($54,400) and community non-profit ($42,500) subsectors. By way of comparison, average compensation for the entire economy was approximately $59,800 in 2017 (Imagine Canada 2019). In the same year employment for the whole sector rose by 1.1%, with gains for the para-public sector and non-profit businesses, but some decline in the core community sector.

Statistics Canada data published in 2021 shows that the non-profit sector employs 2.5 million people, 77% of whom are women; there are persistent racial and gender pay gaps in the non-profit sector; and the number of Black people, Indigenous people, and people of colour employed in the non-profit sector is growing (Jensen 2021). A key component of the Canadian paid and unpaid labour market is found in the non-profit sector.

The Role and Impact of Volunteers

The vital contributions of volunteers in the non-profit sector have long been recognized. Non-profit and voluntary organizations are vehicles for citizen engagement, and the interests, talents, and energies of individual Canadians drive non-profit and voluntary organizations. Virtually all organizations are governed by boards of volunteer directors, which define the missions and objectives of these organizations, and more than half run completely through the donations of volunteers in the forms of both time and money (Statistics Canada 2004).

The economic value of volunteering is also substantial. A 2010 report by TD Economics found that volunteering created $50 billion in economic value for Canadians, and that 13.3 million people volunteered, representing 2.1 billion hours or the equivalent of 1.1 million full-time jobs (Alexander and Gulati 2013). For the year 2013, according to Statistics Canada (2019b), volunteering would have added an extra $41.8 billion to economic activity, or nearly a quarter of the non-profit sector's GDP. The largest single portion of the economic contribution of volunteering occurred in culture and recreation (23.7%), followed by social services (19.7%) and education and research (15.1%).

Volunteering in Canada (Vézina and Crompton 2012) analyzed the volunteer activities of Canadians during the twelve months preceding the 2010 Canada Survey of Giving, Volunteering, and Participating. During that time 13.3 million people, or 47% of those aged 15 and over, volunteered, a significant increase over previous years. Many who got involved were influenced by family or friends who volunteered, but the frequency of finding opportunities through the internet was also growing. Significantly, 10% of these volunteers contributed more than half of the total hours. Most of this volunteer support went to sports and recreation and to social services.

The *State of the Sector* report (Government of Ontario 2013) provided some useful details on the role of volunteers on Ontario's non-profit sector. Volunteers were reported to contribute an average of 161 hours each year, for an overall total of more than 215,000 full-time equivalent positions across the province. While all nonprofits reporting had volunteers serving on their boards, most respondents said they also engaged volunteers in other ways, and 40% of organizations participating in this survey said they were completely volunteer run. Volunteer labour constitutes a substantive contribution to public benefit and is a major source of savings for neoliberal governments seeking to reduce the state's social responsibilities.

Working Conditions and Human Resource Challenges

Human resources issues in the non-profit sector have been the focus of a number of studies and policy initiatives over the past two decades. In 2004, the Canadian Policy Research Networks published a comprehensive report on human resource issues in the non-profit sector (Saunders 2004), making use of Statistics Canada's Workplace and Employee Survey. One issue highlighted in the report was the importance of the particular needs and aspirations of women regarding their workplace, given their overrepresentation in the sector. The demand for flexible work schedules, such as flexible hours and part-time work, was higher in the non-profit sector, and university-educated women were more likely than university-educated men to value respect and commitment in the employer-employee relationship and to prioritize good communication and workplace relations.

The report also noted that in many respects, working conditions in the non-profit sector were above average: the percentage of employees with access to some types of benefits for full-time employees, flexible work hours, and training was higher than in the for-profit sector. However, there was more temporary work in the sector (associated with reduced job security); there were more concerns about the adequacy of training; and fewer opportunities for advancement existed than in other sectors. There was also much lower pay for managers and professionals (especially in comparison with the para-public sector such as schools, hospitals, universities, and colleges). Access to benefits and training opportunities was also better in para-public organizations.

Ron Saunders observed as well that problems of precarious employment and lower pay were reflections of the difficult challenges facing many non-profit organizations: increased responsibilities with less funding and a shift in the nature of funding from long-term support for core services to a focus on short-term funding for specific projects. This situation has greatly increased the precariousness of the non-profit sector (Shields, Cunningham, and Baines 2017).

The importance of human resource issues was highlighted by one of the outcomes of the Voluntary Sector Initiative (VSI), a partnership between the federal governments and representatives of the non-profit sector. The HR Council for the Voluntary and Non-profit Sector, established through the VSI, had a relatively short but active lifespan and was retired in 2018.[5] However, a collaboration between Community Foundations of Canada (CFC) and Imagine Canada is relaunching the legacy of web-based resources from the HR Council. The Ontario Nonprofit Network (ONN) has committed to furthering the "decent work movement" by posting its own resources to this new site (Imagine Canada 2020b).

---

5   The legacy of the VSI is explored in more detail in Chapter 4.

The report *Shaping the Future* (McIsaac, Park, and Toupin 2013) drew on an Ontario-wide survey of 800 non-profit sector leaders to examine the challenges and opportunities of human capital renewal in the sector. It was prepared as part of the ONN's Human Capital Renewal Strategy. The study identified five main areas of concern and, for each area, some strategic opportunities for ONN's continuing work. The five key areas were: competing to find and keep talent; rethinking the model of leadership; skills and competencies of leadership; where future leadership will come from; and diversity in the non-profit sector. The study also noted that while the non-profit sector is a major force in Ontario's social and economic development, sector-specific research and data were largely unavailable.

At the Senate hearings for the 2019 report on the charitable and non-profit sector, Peter Clutterbuck spoke as a senior community planning consultant with the Social Planning Network of Ontario. He emphasized several human resources challenges in the non-profit sector, including the issue of recruiting the kind of talent needed. With the aging of baby-boomers and those employed in the non-profit sector, younger people are needed as replacements. Research has shown they are attracted by the type of work done in the sector, but relatively low wages and salaries make it difficult for them to choose the sector for employment. The problem is compounded by the difficulties faced by this cohort in escaping the burden of student debt they have acquired to gain the knowledge and skills so desperately needed by the sector. Clutterbuck called on the federal government to intensify its engagement in skills training for the social service and public benefit sector (Clutterbuck 2019).

At the same hearings, Professor John Shields, speaking as an expert witness, commented on working conditions within the sector, as well as the kinds of human resource challenges reported by Clutterbuck. Both Clutterbuck and Shields noted that average compensation for full-time equivalent work in 2017 in the core non-profit sector was $42,500, while the average for the entire economy was $59,800. This gap, Shields noted, represents a $17,300 discount for the sector. Shields also noted that core non-profit sector employees, compared to other sectors, also fall behind regarding job security, benefits, and benefits such as pensions. Other employment-related challenges include significant recruitment and retention issues due to non-competitive wages, lack of job security, and lack of career mobility paths within the sector due to relatively flat organizational structures. As noted by Shields, these are very lean organizations.

Shields also elaborated on the personnel challenges reported by Clutterbuck. Leadership in the sector is aging rapidly, with a large percentage of executive directors and other senior managers expected to leave the sector in the next few years. With no obvious replacements, the sector faces the serious problems of a pending leadership gap and loss of institutional memory, a situation that has reached crisis proportions in the wake of the COVID-19 pandemic.

Other human resource challenges reported by Shields include issues of morale, burnout, unpaid overtime, and health issues brought on by stress. As well, the workforce composition is heavily female, and apart from the immigrant settlement services and personal health care areas, it lags behind in terms of ethnic and racial diversity. This leaves the question of how the sector will engage the next generation of workers and the changing demographic profile of the populations it serves.

Along with these serious challenges, there are also important reform initiatives involving both non-profit umbrella organizations and various foundations. The ONN, for example, has developed the Decent Work campaign in the sector to improve pay levels, benefits, and working conditions — with funding support from Atkinson Foundation and Status of Women Canada (ONN n.d.a.).

The Maytree Foundation notes that the new work-from-home culture has shifted employees' needs to evaluate more practical benefits like retirement savings plans and that competing against well-funded companies with extensive compensation benefits can make it challenging for non-profit organizations to attract and retain skilled staff. Maytree has been working with other partners to create the Common Good Plan, a nationally portable workplace savings and retirement program for workers in the non-profit sector. The Common Good Plan is provided by Common Wealth Retirement, a Toronto-based fintech company on a mission to make it possible for every Canadian to achieve a financially secure retirement. The company is working in partnership with a coalition of philanthropic funders and non-profit sector leaders, including Vancity, the Hamilton Community Foundation, and the Metcalf Foundation, as well as Maytree (Stadelmann-Elder 2021).

Precarious Labour and the Contract Funding Regime

Precarious Labour

The employment profile of the core non-profit sector — those community organizations serving the most vulnerable populations and communities — places the sector in the vanguard of the shift away from so-called "standard" employment norms. Full-time permanent employment with decent pay and benefits is replaced by precarious and poorly compensated employment forms that characterize the emerging labour market. The labour market precarity of the workers in the core non-profit sector matches the precarity of living conditions for the sector's clients — in keeping with the fact that the sector's workforce is generally heavily drawn from communities it serves (Baines, Campey, Cunningham, and Shields 2014; Procyk, Lewchuk, and Shields 2017).

Precarity can be understood as the condition of a lack of security and predictability and is associated with the growth of temporary, short-term and other forms of insecure work, as well as low pay and poor or no employment benefits. As well, a significant portion of the work of the sector is carried out by the non-paid work of volunteers along with staff performing many hours of extra non-paid labour to meet obligations to "do more with less." These problems have been magnified by stagnant wages due to years of government austerity following the economic crisis of 2009 and at best, flatlined contract budgets. This has meant an intensification of work without compensation increases in the context of greater societal need for services, contributing significantly to employee demoralization, burnout, and workplace stress, sickness, and injury (Baines et al. 2014; Joy and Shields 2020). In addition, the labour force of the core non-profit sector, as with much of the non-profit and charitable sector in general, is overwhelmingly comprised of female labour, whose pay and benefit compensation are significantly below public and private sector norms (Shields, Cunningham, and Baines 2017).

Findings from the *State of the Sector* survey conducted in 2012–13 (Government of Ontario 2013) confirm these patterns of precarious employment. Less than half of the workers in the sector — about 48% — were considered full time. Of that, 30% were part-time and 21% were short-term employees.

Given that all workers rely for their employment on a model of funding that involves their agencies competing for short-term program contract financing, even so-called full-time workers in the core sector lack security of employment. They are all dependent upon the success of the next contract, which is often not confirmed until quite late in the funding application process. The reality is that these workers are, in essence, permanently temporary (Shields 2014). Their wages or salaries depend on government funding contracts, usually short term and often involving funds delivered after the contractual terms specify the start date for the services funded. Precarity in employment relates to the lack of predictability and security in work, with negative repercussions for both the material and psychological well-being of those employed. The core non-profit sector is rife with such insecurity, experienced by front-line workers as well as by support staff and managers, who are all highly dependent on short-term contract financing of their programs.

The Contract Funding Regime

Around twenty years ago, analysts of the Canadian non-profit sector began to identify the contract funding regime as a major structural problem. *The Capacity to Serve: A Qualitative Study of the Challenges Facing Canada's Non-profit and Voluntary Organizations* noted that "challenges to structural capacity are largely the result of dependence on project-based, time-limited funding that does not support organizational infrastructure" (Canadian Centre for Philanthropy 2003). Since that time, the destructive effects of the contract funding regime have been documented and analyzed by numerous scholars, researchers, and community leaders.[6]

The contract funding regime is integral to the neoliberal restructuring of state-funded human services. With this system, programs are funded through rigid short-term contracts that must be bid on competitively between nonprofits and, possibly, for-profit organizations. There are strict limitations on how funded dollars are to be spent, greatly reducing costing flexibility. Moreover, funding is inadequate to cover the full costs of delivering the contracted services, much less the general costs associated with administration and community outreach.

---

6   See for example Chambon, and Richmond 2000a, 2000b; Scott 2003; Saunders 2004; Eakin and Richmond 2004), Richmond and Shields 2004; Shields 2005; Evans, Richmond, and Shields 2005; Gibson, O'Donnell, and Rideout. 2007; Elson 2011; Baines et al. 2014; and Joy and Shields 2020.

Funders expect volunteers and donations (and another forms of community support) to fill the funding gap (Eakin and Richmond 2004; Joy and Shields 2020). Furthermore, the unpredictability of funding makes even so-called full-time jobs precarious since, if contracts do not come through, these jobs will be lost. Contract funding in fact structures precarity into the very fabric of the non-profit labour force, effectively making most of the jobs in the sector "permanently temporary."

A revealing documentation of the multitude of problems associated with contract funding was provided by Kerri Gibson, Susan O'Donnell, and Vanda Rideout (2007). These included burdensome and bureaucratic accountability and reporting requirements that decreased the time for community service, and the further reduction of front-line service delivery with staff time diverted to writing complex and detailed grant proposals to justify further funding for even established programs. The research also verified that short-term contract funding creates funding gaps, financial instability, and frequent failures to meet payroll without bridging from other funding sources or organizational reserves. Contract funding is therefore associated closely with insecure and underpaid work for those employed in the sector.

The contract funding system also enables the neoliberal state to control aspects of non-profit organizations' operations from a distance. This is the so-called process of "centralized decentralization." Without directly legislating control over nonprofits, control is indirectly exercised through the terms of a financial contract that spells out in detail how services are to be delivered and managed. Hence, market-based contracts cement considerable control by state funders over non-profit service provision. This control is reinforced through strict accountability, reporting, and auditing measures by the funder (Evans and Shields 2010). This is also a primary way in which neoliberal market-based values are transferred to the non-profit sector, what Taylor calls a "cultural take-over by stealth" (2002, 98–99).

We continue to see that the problems associated with contract funding remain acute for many nonprofits. In a report from anti-violence experts intended to assist the federal government in developing a national action plan on gender-based violence, specific mention was made of the need for core funding for community-based organizations: "Providing community organizations with stable funding will enable them to implement programs that are long-lasting and therefore more useful and effective" (Hayes 2021). Shields (2019) is among those who emphasize that practical reforms of the contract funding regime are not only necessary but also possible:

> On a pragmatic level, what can government funders do to address this situation? I would suggest three things: One, they can introduce longer-term contracts based upon performance. In fact, we already see this happening in the federal government in terms of IRCC, which in its latest funding cycle has issued five-year proposals, five-year contracts for organizations to bid on.
>
> Second, funders can reduce overly rigid rules regarding how contract dollars are spent in delivering programs. This can reduce overhead costs and excessive staff time spent on administration and increasing the flexibility for service improvement. In other words, even without more dollars, better dollars or more flexible dollars can do a lot to help the sector.
>
> Third, in terms of costing contracts, funders should include financing that provides a living wage for workers within the sector. All of this would go a significant distance to increasing job security, employment predictability and improving employment conditions in the core non-profit sector.

A September 2023 LinkedIn posting by Tyler Colbourne, executive director at Healthy Minds Cooperative, accurately describes the problems of contract funding:

> Today I saw a posting for an Executive Director position in the HRM. The salary is $31,000/year, for 30 hours a week. Responsibilities include leadership and management, financial management, diversity and inclusion, stewardship and fundraising, human resources, facility and operations management, marketing, governance support for a board of directors, and likely volunteer management. This is unreasonable and unfair…. It is disheartening to see non-profits pay so little but expect so much. No wonder so many people leave the sector. We can do better. I have worked with plenty of non-profits that are committed to a living

wage and advocating to partners, funders, and stakeholders the importance of paying people fairly. The sector needs a shake-up before everyone burns out and quits.

Accountability and Evaluation

Along with contract funding comes a system of accountability that involves tightly controlled obligations regarding how funding is directed and spent. It is a system of purely administrative accountability, rigorously monitored, with detailed reporting requirements designed with the goal of ensuring "efficiency" and "value for money" for government spending (Joy and Shields 2016). As mentioned, these reporting techniques provide for state control, at a distance, of non-profit service providers (Shields and Evans 1998). But this system does not recognize that these organizations actually have multiple accountabilities. Responsibility to funders is very important but no more so than accountability to the broader public and to the clients and communities they serve. There are also multiple other parties requiring appropriate accountability processes, including boards, members, volunteers, paid staff, donors, and partners. Neoliberal accountability frameworks operate against this diverse and democratic non-profit accountability structure; under neoliberal governance, accountability to funders trumps all other forms of accountability.

Government and funders have embraced the simplistic notion that administrative accountability equates to public accountability, when in fact the two are quite different. Administrative accounting involves competent and timely reporting by nonprofits on how the funds are spent according to the conditions attached to the grant or contract. Public accountability is the responsibility of the funders and governments and concerns the obligation to provide the funds necessary for health and social services and to communicate this information clearly to the general public (Shields 2005). One of the serious negative impacts of contract funding "accountability" is the loss of the autonomy that non-profit service agencies require to shape programs and assign resources according to community needs (Lowe, Richmond, and Shields 2017). Autonomy is crucial for nonprofits in fulfilling their community service and advocacy missions (Omidvar and Richmond 2003).

Confounding administrative accountability with meaningful assessment of program results has led to further confusion — deliberate or otherwise — with respect to the nature of evaluation. The complex system of administrative reporting imposed with contract funding is frequently justified by funders with simplistic sloganeering, such as "the taxpayer has a right to know how the money is being spent." Peter Aucoin (2005) observed in a Treasury Board discussion paper on program evaluation and decision-making that federal perspectives and priorities (as with contract funding and administrative accountability) have evolved according to the imperatives of neoliberal "results-based management."

Evaluation is inherently political with respect to the topics chosen for assessment, the methods employed, and the interpretation of the findings. It involves both value judgements and power relations, especially the power of funders over other parties involved in delivering services and assessing their results. The conflation of the notions of "accountability" and "evaluation" places a near-impossible burden on nonprofits and institutionalizes the funders' general abandonment of responsibility for providing the resources necessary to evaluate the long-term outcomes of publicly funded health and social services (Chambon and Richmond 2000a, 2000b).

John Mayne (2001) noted that proper evaluations are inherently labour intensive, time consuming, and consequently expensive. The measurement of "outcomes" and longer-term results requires significant resources in terms of time and professional expertise:

> It is possible, and reasonable to expect, that nonprofits provide funders with a reasonable level of accountability. But it is simply impossible at an agency level — in spite of persistent efforts to pretend otherwise — to provide true evaluation of the long-term impact of the services provided. Such an evaluation requires, at a minimum, multi-agency collaboration facilitated by one or more funders, involvement of evaluation experts and other researchers with knowledge of the relevant economic and demographic characteristics of the clientele, and a multi-year time frame. All this in turn depends on significant amounts of dedicated funding which are essentially permanently unavailable. (Shields 2005)

Under neoliberalism and new public management, accountability has been employed as a tool to control service contracts and their operation and as a way to impose neoliberal market values upon the non-profit sector.

Resilience in the Face of Adversity

In spite of the many challenges faced by the non-profit sector, it has proved remarkably resilient over the past decades. The capacity of the sector to do "more with less" is renowned, driven by the dedication of its staff to an ethos of caring and giving. Nonprofits have proven to be remarkably good at adjusting to adversity and difficult conditions in order to fulfill their missions. The lean funding realities faced by the sector present substantial challenges for capacity building for non-profit organizations, making it difficult for forward planning and especially for managing through crisis situations.

Flexible responses to an ever-changing funding environment have allowed the sector to generally maintain its activities and sometimes to expand them but under continuous stress.[7] Maintaining a diversity of funding sources has been key to this success, with the provinces providing the largest portion of government revenues in both the core and para-public sectors, and foundations donating vital resources for emerging issues.

Nonprofits have more than proven their worth in Canadian society. They continue to represent a substantial portion of Canada's economic activity. Equally important — perhaps more — is their role as a vital component of health and social services, particularly for the most vulnerable communities. Canadians have demonstrated their support by contributing impressive amounts of volunteer time as well as monetary donations. Nevertheless, there are important warning signs of growing divisions within the sector. An increasing number of foundation grants are very large and go primarily to para-public sector charities. The imposition of contract funding on the core sector has left its staff in a situation of permanently temporary employment and further heightened the disparities between the core and para-public sectors. Precarious funding and employment in the core sector undermine its effectiveness as well as the survivability of many organizations and the services to the communities they serve. The contract funding regime also threatens the vital role of nonprofits in advocacy — a subject we address in the next chapter.

---

7   Data used in the chapter mostly predates the impact of COVID-19 on sector finances and activities. This will be reviewed in the fifth chapter of this book.

CHAPTER 4

The Essential Role of Non-profit Advocacy

In addition to their commitment to service as mission-driven organizations, the other prime role of nonprofits is that of advocacy. The sector's engagement in society to fulfil missions and advance social justice causes has long been recognized as essential to enhancing the liberal democratic experience in society. At the height of the expansion of the welfare state in Canada in the later 1960s to the mid-1970s, governments recognized the importance of non-profit organizations' advocacy, even in some cases funding them in support of this role. The idea of advocacy is often conceptualized as one of expressing "community voice," with non-profit service providers strategically placed to speak to the needs of clients from vulnerable communities.

Advocacy is sometimes direct, as in the case of "big advocacy," in terms of publicly taking stances on major policy issues and even challenging government. But more often we see cases of "small advocacy," involving the everyday interactions and consultations that non-profit staff and their umbrella organizations have with funders and other government officials. Both forms of advocacy are important for the policy process (Evans and Shields 2014).

Under neoliberal forms of governance, however, there have been fundamental changes in government attitudes towards non-profit advocacy. Neoliberalism casts the sector one-dimensionally, as no more than a cheap and compliant source of service provision that can aid in shrinking the size and scope of the state (Shields and Evans 1998). This kind of "partnership" model contributes to a "depoliticization" of the sector. In fact, neoliberalism views advocacy work as "special interest" activity that should *not* be funded, especially if the activity is critical of the government's own policies. Neoliberalism's negative position toward nonprofits that engage in advocacy, even if such activity is funded with independent resources, casts such organizations in their view as untrustworthy. In essence, neoliberalism seeks to negate the progressive advocacy/voice role of non-profit organizations, an anti-democratic move (Evans and Shields 2018).

Neoliberalism has always been suspicious of, and less than welcoming to, non-profit advocacy activities. Meaningful engagement by nonprofits in the policy process requires a degree of acceptance by the state of the legitimacy of their advocacy efforts. The hostility to non-profit advocacy was especially prominent during the latter part of the federal Conservative Harper administration, when the government challenged the charitable status of many organizations advocating around various Conservative policy positions, such as on energy and global warming (Beeby 2014). In such an environment, the problem of "advocacy chill" within the non-profit sector grew especially acute and often muted or even silenced the voices of government-funded community service providers.

Nevertheless, many nonprofits, including some largely dependent on government contracts, continue to use advocacy to promote an alternative social justice voice. They continue to speak out for domestic and international environmental justice and human rights and for progressive social policies, and in opposition to the harmful impacts of neoliberalism. These activities take a multitude of forms and create various tensions — including determined opposition from governments at all levels.

In the 2017 book *The Shifting Terrain: Non-profit Policy Advocacy in Canada,* Nick Mulé and Gloria Desantis provide a general analysis of the state of community-based and non-profit advocacy in Canada today, along with a number of selected case studies at the provincial and local levels. They note that advocacy has always been a core function of the non-profit sector but remains one of the most contentious aspects of government and non-profit sector relations. Growing government hostility to non-profit advocacy in Canada goes back more than two decades but took a decisive turn in 2006, when the federal government began to eliminate or drastically reduce the funding for organizations advocating for progressive policies. More recently, many provincial governments followed the federal lead with funding cuts for progressive organizations (Mulé and Desantis 2017, 4). And in 2012 the federal government's announcement that a number of nonprofits had been selected for Canada Revenue Agency (CRA) audits intensified the general climate of advocacy chill (Cameron and Kwiecien 2019).

Mulé and Desantis (2017, 6–24) focus on policy advocacy and view it as a form of citizen engagement in which nonprofits play a vital role. They note that the neoliberal outlook that dominates Western liberal democracies has produced a shift to market-driven policy governance that either controls and contains the voices of the non-profit sector or excludes them completely. In their concluding chapter, they describe advocacy as an important way of promoting social justice through the interaction of civil society and state actors. The authors also see the trend to reduction of funding for nonprofits, or even outright de-funding of advocacy organizations, as curtailing advocacy activities in two important ways: directly for the organizations whose funding is cut or eliminated, and indirectly through advocacy chill. In spite of these obstacles, they conclude that the non-profit sector and the communities it serves continue to find ways to reform public policy and strengthen democracy through their innovative advocacy efforts.

The Voluntary Sector Initiative

The Voluntary Sector Initiative (VSI) was an important episode in the history of relations between Canadian nonprofits and the federal government. Representatives from both sides devoted considerable time to these efforts, and the easing of restrictions on advocacy was one of the main goals of the non-profit sector. The VSI experience is important in terms of what was accomplished and even more significant with respect to what was not. This was a point in time when Canadian nonprofits had not only become objectively/materially a distinctive and substantive force in society but subjectively were gaining consciousness of this reality. The VSI marked a formative moment when non-profit organizations as a sector began expressing this voice. However, the VSI also sheds light on the challenges that can arise within the non-profit sector in realizing this. The diversity of the sector made the achievement of single unified voice challenging, and it was ultimately unsuccessful.

What Took Place?

Kathy Brock (2004), Peter Elson (2011), and Rachel Laforest (2011b) detail the unfolding of the VSI process, which grew out of two reports by different bodies. The Panel on Accountability and Governance in the Voluntary Sector (1999) was an initiative of the non-profit sector that produced *Building on Strength: Improving Governance and*

Accountability in Canada's Voluntary Sector (the so-called Broadbent Report). This outlined the need for the sector both to improve its own operations and to strengthen relations with business and government. As well, representatives of the federal government along with selected leaders from the sector produced *Working Together: Report of the Joint Tables*, which recommended several joint tables to frame the negotiations between the two sectors, structured by the Coordinating Committee (Government of Canada and Voluntary Sector 1999). In June 2000 the federal government responded by announcing the creation of the VSI. There was $94.6 million allocated over five years for the work of the seven joint tables: Coordinating Committee, Accord, Awareness, Capacity, Information Management and Technology, Regulatory, and National Volunteerism Initiative. The non-profit sector created and funded two more working groups on the issues seen as most important: funding and advocacy. These were two areas that the federal government refused to take a formal part in (Elson and Carmichael 2022).

The VSI became a major effort, intended to alter the relationship between non-profit actors and federal government departments engaged in interactions with the sector. The intent was to place the relationship on a respectful basis guided by a code of conduct. Sector representation for the VSI came from a steering group of senior representatives, and the federal side was coordinated by the Voluntary Sector Task Force, located within the Privy Council Office. Much of the $94.6 million allocated to this initiative went to the departments providing support to the joint tables (Harper 2023).

In order to speed up the process, the Joint Accord Table adapted "compacts" that had been negotiated recently in England and Scotland. The draft Accord was ready by May 2001 and submitted to extensive public consultations, but the final draft remained much the same as the original. The Accord was a statement of general principles, although it did attempt to legitimize policy advocacy by the sector. Specific direction was intended to come from the Code of Good Practice on Policy Dialogue and the Code of Good Practice on Funding, to help provide direction for enhancing sector participation in policy development and to improve funding practices. Significantly, the Funding Code was supposed to guarantee funding for activities including research, capital expenditures, innovation, policy dialogue, and advocacy (Laforest 2011b).

What Was Accomplished?

Brock (2004) discusses the Joint Regulatory Table (JRT), which began operating after the signing of the Accord and brought together representatives of federal departments to examine, with sector input, possible changes in regulatory mechanisms identified through the VSI process. Relatively little was accomplished by the JRT, for various reasons, particularly the decision of government representatives to treat the two issues most important to the sector, funding and advocacy, as "off the table." The JRT report did produce immediate responses in the following areas: a simplified tax form for charities; a streamlined registration process for obtaining charitable status; a commitment by the CRA to make policies more transparent and accessible through web postings; and new policy guidelines on the permissible business activities of charities. The 2004 federal budget pledged $12 million per year to improve charity regulation and to enact most of the JRT's recommendations, with the exception of three dealing with appeals on decisions about charitable status.

Laforest (2011b, 84–86) identifies a number of immediate gains for the sector from the VSI process. The National Volunteerism Joint Table initiated the Canada Volunteerism Initiative and in this process provided funding for two large and well-established pan-Canadian organizations, Volunteer Canada and the Canadian Centre for Philanthropy, to establish provincial and local networks throughout Canada. The Information Management/Information Technology Joint Table launched a web portal for the voluntary sector through a pan-Canadian consortium of voluntary organizations, led by the Association of Canadian Community Colleges. The Capacity Joint Table initiated a number of activities, including funding the Coalition of National Voluntary Organizations and the Association of Canadian Community Colleges to lead the National Learning Initiative, intended to promote effective leadership in the non-profit sector, as well as the Policy Internships and Fellowships program, which placed voluntary sector personnel inside the federal bureaucracy and civil servants inside the non-profit sector.

Brock (2004) sees the most important accomplishment of the VSI as the embedding and institutionalization of links between the sector and the federal government, potentially leading to gradual but constant improvements in relations over time. Other scholars are more critical. Elson (2011, 56–77) identifies some limited successes from the initiative and a larger number of setbacks or failures. He states that the two codes produced by the effort (on policy dialogue and funding) "were entirely process-focused and provided no defensible or accountable criteria that could be used to hold either the voluntary sector or the government to account." He concludes as well that non-achievement of a new definition of charity was one of the important failures of the VSI.

Laforest (2011b, 86–89), whose research included extensive interviews with sector leaders, is also critical of the VSI experience. The main benefits, in her view, lay in the sector gaining greater visibility and credibility with respect to key issues and the general importance of non-profit organizations in society by government and the public. As well, the process gave sector leaders valuable experience (both positive and negative) in negotiating with government representatives. An important drawback, however, was that for some time the advocacy efforts of the sector were focused almost exclusively on relations with the federal government. Laforest also notes that the structures of the VSI favoured the representation of the larger and better-funded non-profit organizations, giving rise to "elite accommodation." Smaller organizations, even those with direct representation in the process, often felt marginalized, and there was widespread dissatisfaction among those organizations with the amount of money going to a few large organizations. Laforest observes that the process included ongoing and serious tensions over the naming of the sector ("voluntary" versus "voluntary and community," for example), reflecting the belief among many sector leaders that the "voluntary" designation excluded the numerous non-profit organizations that were, in fact, not volunteer-based.

Another important outcome of the VSI process, initiated by the Capacity Joint Table, was the publication in 2004 of the *National Survey on Non-profit and Voluntary Organizations and the Satellite Account of Non-profit Institutions and Volunteering*. This represented a huge gain for the sector, institutionalizing the concept of a distinct component of the Canadian economy and its health and social service systems that was neither "public" nor "private" and providing the first reliable source of pan-Canadian data on the size, scope, and activities of the sector. Ultimately, however, this step was followed by an important failure of government to honour its own accords. Although meant to be an ongoing process with collaboration between Statistics Canada and various foundations and non-profit organizations, no sector-focused pan-Canadian survey of its size and scale was ever repeated, although much more modest surveys of the sector have appeared occasionally. We know that what gets measured is an indication of the value placed on it. The statistical neglect of the sector is an indication of the secondary importance placed on it by the government. Consequently, our measurements and understandings of the non-profit sector remain incomplete.

Lessons from the VSI Experience

Patrick Johnston (2013, 21) provides some useful insights concerning the VSI experience from his perspective as a direct participant in the process:

> The VSI was, without doubt, the most ambitious and comprehensive attempt ever made to strengthen the relationship between Canada's voluntary sector and the federal government. It accomplished a great deal. But the VSI also fell short of the high hopes and expectations that had been placed on it.

Johnston sees the main achievements of the VSI in the formalization of federal government commitments to improve relations with and to materially support the non-profit sector. This commitment was formalized in the Accord between the Government of Canada and the voluntary sector, signed and unveiled by Prime Minister Chrétien at a public ceremony in 2001. Unfortunately, the Harper government, which soon replaced the Liberals, wanted to be completely disassociated from the Accord, and many of the related commitments to the sector never were realized.

As for the flaws in the VSI process, Johnston (2013) identifies many, for the sector itself as well as the federal government. The non-profit representatives had little understanding of the complex operations of the federal government, just as their government counterparts were relatively ignorant of the workings of nonprofits. The consultative process of the VSI could not negate the fundamental power imbalance between the two groups involved. The diversity of the non-profit sector, while generally a source of strength, in this case became a major obstacle to developing a common narrative. Finally, as observed by other scholars and commentators, the fact that the funding for sector representation flowed mainly to larger pan-Canadian organizations became a source of division for the sector.

Mulé and Desantis (2017, 12) note that while the VSI process raised strong hopes in the non-profit sector that the issue of advocacy would be taken more seriously, the experiences they documented suggest the opposite. This is confirmed by numerous personal conversations with sector leaders.[1] Many years after the VSI, veterans of non-profit advocacy efforts still feel bitter about the time they invested and the promises that were made compared to the results achieved.

There are several important reasons for the failure of the VSI to achieve lasting progress on the issues most important to the non-profit sector. One was the resistance of federal government representatives during the process of the VSI to deal in a substantial way with the fundamental issues of funding and advocacy. Another was the fact that the goals of sector leaders clashed with the neoliberal ideology of the Liberal government of the time: specifically, the commitment of the Liberal government to reducing public expenses and delivering more services, at less cost, through the "charitable" or "voluntary" sector (Elson 2011, 104–105). A third was difficulty of the sector in achieving a common and strong political voice, specifically the tensions between thousands of smaller grassroots organizations, particularly community-based health and social service organizations, and the leadership of the larger pan-Canadian organizations selected and funded by the federal government to represent the non-profit sector as a whole.

The flawed character of non-profit representation in the VSI initiative has been described in the following way:

> There was a representational disconnect at the VSI between what was needed to advance public policy in a formal institution like the federal government and the number and range of people who were called on from all parts of Canada to participate in numerous joint working groups, many with little or no policy expertise. Compounding this representational deficit was the marked absence of provincial or municipal government representatives, sector leaders from Quebec, and meaningful representation from racialized, Black, and Indigenous communities. These relational disconnects led to the absence of political legitimacy for the sector and for the process as a whole.

---

1 Private conversations with Ted Richmond and John Shields

> Relationship lesson: The greatest political credibility will come with groups that have both policy expertise and broad and deep networks that reach into communities. (Elson and Carmichael 2022)

Nevertheless, the legacy of the issues and the non-profit mobilization from this period live on. Many sector leaders took a self-reflective and critical look at their own style of advocacy and developed new and more active or inclusive approaches. Some sector-specific organizations took advantage of the opening towards policy dialogue in their own ways. The various settlement umbrella organizations across Canada, for example, organized two successful National Settlement Conferences with support from Citizenship and Immigration Canada — now Immigration, Refugees and Citizenship Canada (IRCC) — with participation from academic immigration researchers, provincial and municipal representatives, and grassroots settlement providers. And the funding issue and its links with advocacy continue to be negotiated, sometimes with modest success, at the municipal and provincial levels and especially with federal departments. In particular, the VSI experience was a catalyst for the development of provincial non-profit umbrella organizations (Elson and Carmichael 2022).

Regulation of Charitable Activities and Advocacy Chill

The regulation of charitable activities and the associated restrictions on advocacy efforts have been a major and long-standing issue for the non-profit sector in Canada. Elson (2011, 13–14) identifies this as one of three core issues for the sector for more than thirty years — along with the capacity to advocate in the public interest and the role of the sector in service provision. Charity laws in Canada, and their administration, are complex subjects, and Elson (2011, 40–43) lists fourteen major changes in Canada's charity laws between 1948 and 2007. Since the political activities of charities remained persistently contentious, and about half of Canada's nonprofits are registered charities, the real or perceived restrictions on advocacy — as defined in the Income Tax Act (ITA) and administered by the federal Canada Revenue Agency (CRA) — have historically been of concern.

Many of the issues reviewed by Elson were taken up again in the hearings and final report of the Special Senate Committee on the Charitable Sector (Special Senate Committee on the Charitable Sector 2019, 84). Others were new or received increased attention. Witnesses testifying to the committee identified comprehensive review and reform of the ITA provisions governing the behaviour of registered charities as a major priority. More specifically, there were five key areas for reform identified: categories of registered charity; political activities; business activities; the direction and control/own activities rules; and the "no gift to non-qualified donees" rule.

Recommendation 27 from the report was for the Government of Canada to replace the categories of registered charity with two new categories: public charity and private charity, rather than the current three categories of registered charity: charitable organizations, public foundations, and private foundations.

With respect to political activities by charities, the report noted that the federal government had been engaged in active study and consultations on the issue for many years and had already initiated key reforms. Bill C-86, which received Royal Assent in December 2018, contained measures which enable a charity to be involved in "public policy dialogue and development activities" without limitation, so long as the activities further the organization's stated charitable purpose. At the same time the legislation maintains the prohibition on charities providing "direct or indirect support of, or opposition to, any political party or candidate for public office." The report also notes that in January 2019, the CRA issued draft administrative guidance on public policy dialogue and development activities by charities. This guidance interprets the ITA, as amended by Bill C-86, to allow "a charity to fully engage without limitation in [public policy dialogue and development activities] that further its stated charitable purposes provided they never directly or indirectly support or oppose a political party or candidate for public office." The draft guidance also addresses the meaning of "direct or indirect support" (Government of Canada 2019, 86).

With respect to business activities, Recommendation 28 calls on the Government of Canada to direct the CRA to develop and implement a pilot project to assess the viability of granting registered charities greater latitude in undertaking revenue-generating activities (provided the proceeds are used to further charitable purposes) through the implementation of a "destination of funds" test (92). Recommendation 29 asks the government to direct the CRA to update policy statement CPS-019 ("What is a related business") to provide greater clarity on permissible revenue generation activities for registered charities, particularly with regard to revenue generating opportunities arising from new technologies.

Recommendation 30 requests that the Government of Canada directs the CRA to revise Guidance CG-002 "Canadian registered charities carrying out activities outside Canada." The revised guidance should demonstrate a shift in focus from "direction and control" to careful monitoring through the implementation of an "expenditure responsibility test." Witnesses reported that the practice of the CRA in this regard was problematic, particularly for international aid organizations seeking equitable partnerships with non-Canadian organizations.

The understanding and interpretation of the "no gifts to non-qualified donees rule" has meant that charitable organizations can provide a gift of money or goods to another organization so that the other organization can fulfil its objects only if the other organization is a qualified donee. A transfer of funds to a non-qualified donee is cause for revocation of charitable status. Witnesses reported this as highly problematic for Canadian charities developing partnerships based on equality and mutual respect. As reported, for example, in testimony to the Senate hearings, many Indigenous organizations refuse on principle to seek charitable status with its associated forms of external control. Accordingly, Recommendation 31 proposed that the government directs the CRA to develop, implement, and evaluate a pilot project to allow registered charities to make gifts to non-qualified donees in certain limited circumstances, namely where the gifted funds are subject to careful monitoring and used for exclusively charitable purposes, in order to facilitate cooperation between registered charities and non-charities (99).

Two additional recommendations related to the ongoing responsibilities of the federal government in regularly reviewing the provisions of the ITA and its interpretation by the CRA. Recommendation 32 proposes that the Government of Canada reviews the ITA provisions governing registered charities every five years, beginning no later than next fiscal year. Recommendation 33 proposes that the government considers which activities registered charities should not be allowed to carry out and proscribe them through precisely defined statutory prohibitions (100).

Imagine Canada (2022) highlighted and commended two additional recent initiatives by the federal government in its 2022 budget with respect to regulation of charities. The budget proposed to amend the ITA to allow a charity to provide its resources to organizations that are not qualified donees, provided that accountability requirements are met, thereby implementing the spirit of Bill S-216, The Effective and Accountable Charities Act. The budget also proposed to introduce a new graduated disbursement quota for charities, with the rate increasing from 3.5% to 5% for those with investment assets exceeding $1 million. These proposed changes were to come into effect on or after January 1, 2023, depending on the charity's fiscal period.

Advocacy Chill

Advocacy chill is a serious concern for the non-profit movement in Canada. The attempts of the Stephen Harper government to muzzle environmental and social justice groups through the activities of the CRA may be the most notorious example. History shows, however, that this was only one part of the federal resistance to non-profit advocacy efforts — previous Liberal governments had been eliminating funding for non-profit research and advocacy organizations for several decades (Elson 2011; Mulé and Desantis 2017).

Advocacy efforts may also be restricted or reduced by the promotion of competition for funding for short-term service contracts in the non-profit sector. For non-profit service organizations, the focus moves to efforts with government funders to secure scarce service contracts necessary for the organization's survival, rather than broader mission-based activities. This creates a strong motivation to avoid criticizing government and to "not bite the hand that feeds them."

The constraints on non-profit advocacy go far beyond those related to protecting charitable status; advocacy chill is not limited to charitable organizations (Burrowes and Laforest 2017). Mulé and Desantis (2017, 16–17) identify five main reasons for what they describe as the "soiling of advocacy." These include government rules, the perception and understanding of these rules by non-profit organizations, muzzle clauses in some government funding contracts, personal muzzling of individuals, and government funding cuts for nonprofits. Elson (2011, 26) notes that governments have learned that de facto control over non-profit and voluntary organizations can be achieved with minor financial investment. Contract conditions in even nominal service agreements can effectively limit extra-contractual activities, including independent advocacy.

However, most nonprofits, including charities and government-funded service agencies, continue to carry out advocacy as integral to their mission. These efforts, which often have significant impact, are extremely diverse in nature.

The Many Faces and Forms of Non-profit Advocacy

The advocacy efforts of Canadian nonprofits are extensive and diverse. They are determined mainly by the needs of the communities they serve, in relation to current policies of the federal, provincial, and municipal governments. But they are shaped as well by other key factors, including evolving popular consciousness of critical international and domestic issues (such as climate change and Indigenous rights), the impact of evolving technology on communications, and the organizational and financial imperatives of the non-profit organizations. The forms of advocacy are shaped by various types of networks (including social media) that are accessible to those mobilizing on an issue. Community support and engagement are critical for advocacy, even more so than the type of funding received by the organization. For example, the community legal clinics in Ontario, although entirely funded by the provincial government, have been able to sustain their advocacy efforts on behalf of poor and marginalized communities because of the independence of their community boards.

Umbrella Organizations

Umbrella organizations bring together nonprofits with similar missions and play a major role in advocacy. Along with providing critical member services, including skills training and informational publications, they are well-positioned to speak directly with the appropriate level of government on behalf of their member organizations and the communities they serve. Umbrella organizations often play a central role as well in acquiring resources for key research projects of interest to the non-profit sector and in coordinating their implementation. Advocacy efforts undertaken by umbrella organizations or inside coalitions also play a strategic role in sheltering particular nonprofits from the risk of retaliation by funders for pursuing their critiques of government policies and priorities (Burrowes and Laforest 2017).

An important number of umbrella organizations in Canada operate at the pan-Canadian level. Imagine Canada (2022) describes its mission as working to bolster the Canadian charitable sector's role in building, enriching, and defining our nation. Most pan-Canadian non-profit organizations, including umbrella organizations, are organized on the basis of mission. Examples include CanadaHelps, Canadian Cancer Society, Canadian Red Cross, Cancer Research Society, Cooperation Canada (formerly Canadian Council for International Cooperation), Diabetes Canada, and Volunteer Canada. Foundations often provide support to particular advocacy efforts, or related research initiatives, initiated by pan-Canadian umbrella organizations.

Other pan-Canadian advocacy organizations mobilize around particular issues. The Migrant Rights Network describes itself on its website as a cross-Canada alliance to combat racism and fight for migrant justice. The Black Health Alliance's website describes it as a community-based charitable organization that works to improve the health and well-being of Black communities in Canada. Egale Canada describes itself as a charity that works for a world where every person, regardless of sexual orientation and gender identity, can achieve their complete potential, free from hatred and bias. There is a diversity of organizations doing advocacy for their members' interests as well as providing services; examples include CARP, representing seniors, the Canadian Automobile Association, and trade unions.

A significant amount of policy advocacy also takes place at the provincial level, both in terms of activity and with respect to impact. The provinces provide a large portion of government funding for community-based health and social service organizations. Along with the funding issue, many important social policies are determined mainly at the provincial level, including concerning childcare, housing, and health services, which includes mental health and women's support services.

As at the pan-Canadian level, much of the provincial-focused advocacy work is done through umbrella organizations. The Ontario Nonprofit Network (ONN) is one example of an organization very active in a range of policy issues impacting the non-profit sector. Provincially based umbrella organizations of immigrant- and refugee-serving organizations that are deeply involved at both the federal and provincial levels of government include Affiliation of Multicultural Societies and Service Agencies of BC (AMSSA), Ontario Council of Agencies Serving Immigrants (OCASI), and in Quebec, the Table de concertation des organismes au service des personnes réfugiées et immigrantes (TCRI).

Provincial governments have also followed the VSI example by developing more formal policies and structures for collaboration with the non-profit sector. In 2014, Elson reported that nine of ten provinces made a serious commitment to institutionalizing policy dialogue with the non-profit sector. Many of these initiatives have since faded, as a result of changes in provincial governments and related policies and priorities — but not all. Johnston (2013) gives the example of the government of Ontario in 2011 outlining a strategy to create a stronger partnership with the non-profit sector, in collaboration with the ONN, and subsequently creating a Partnership Project in the Ministry of Citizenship and Immigration (MCI) to advance the strategy. These initiatives led subsequently to the Funding Reform project, intended to streamline the processes associated with grant (transfer payment) applications and administration, thereby reducing unnecessary administrative burdens for nonprofits.[2] With the election of the Progressive Conservative Doug Ford governments in Ontario, non-profit sector relationships with the state were not given priority and the ministry (MCI) focused on non-profit relationships was eliminated.

Member-Funded Advocacy Activities

Another major form of non-profit advocacy in Canada is through member-funded organizations. Whether through paid memberships or supporters' donations, or a combination of both, these kinds of resources make nonprofits less dependent on government funding and therefore less subject to advocacy chill. Many nonprofits receive some portion of their revenues through paid memberships and donations, including most health and social service community organizations, but some organizations with advocacy as a major component of their mission have tailored their fundraising efforts accordingly.

---

2   This latter observation is based on the personal experiences of co-author Ted Richmond, as one of the government staff liaison representatives to the Partnership Projects and the associated efforts for Funding Reform. More recently ONN reports that parts of Funding Reform have stalled (ONN n.d.b).

Many of the environmental organizations operating in Canada depend largely on contributions from supporters. Greenpeace is a notable example. Although now an international organization with many significant "wins" for environmental justice,[3] Greenpeace was founded in Canada in the early 1970s, when it drew widespread support for a voyage to Amchitka, Alaska, protesting the testing of atomic bombs.

Greenpeace, both in Canada and internationally, has frequently faced potential repression of its advocacy activities in the form of lawsuits. In order to maintain independence, Greenpeace limits its funding sources to donors and foundations and also screens donations for potential unwanted influence. For the same reason, Greenpeace Canada is registered as a non-profit rather than a charity, which means that donations are not eligible for income tax credits.

Amnesty International is another international organization with millions of supporters worldwide and strong support in Canada. It views its mission as conducting research and generating action to prevent and end grave abuses of human rights and to demand justice for those whose rights have been violated (website 2022). Amnesty International strives to be impartial, holding all actors to the same obligations as defined in international human rights law and standards. In order to maintain its independence, it relies for funding on donations from individuals and does not accept funding for human rights research and campaigning work from any government.

Advocacy Efforts by Foundations

Canada's private and public foundations play an important role in non-profit advocacy by commissioning and circulating policy research related to the non-profit sector, supporting advocacy efforts by other non-profit organizations, and developing campaigns, on their own or through alliances, on a multitude of vital topics of public interest. The choice of activities to initiate or promote or fund is as diverse as the missions of these foundations. As stated by Philanthropic Foundations Canada (PFC) on its website: "We promote the growth and development of effective and responsible grantmakers in Canada through provision of membership services, resources and advocacy."

---

3   See, for example, Greenpeace 2021.

As discussed earlier in this chapter, a major portion of advocacy efforts by Canadian foundations has focused on CRA rules governing the finances and functioning of charitable organizations. These foundations include[4] the Max Bell Foundation and the Muttart Foundation, both active in reform efforts focused on the legislation and regulations governing advocacy activities by charities. The Max Bell Foundation also delivers programs and supports Canadian charities with grants, with a focus on health and wellness, education, and the environment. The Muttart Foundation believes that Canada is best served through a strong, independent, and interconnected voluntary sector and works with other foundations to support that objective. The foundation has commissioned surveys of Canadians on their views about charities and issues affecting charities and published the results in a series of influential reports, including *Talking About Charities* (2013).

Several Toronto-based foundations focus on promoting economic opportunity and combatting inequality. Maytree Foundation works towards systemic solutions to combat poverty through a human rights approach. Atkinson Foundation is committed to social and economic justice and prioritizes strengthening movements for decent work and a fair economy. Metcalf Foundation focuses on poverty reduction, as well as the environment and the performing arts. Another Toronto foundation, Laidlaw Foundation, supports young people being healthy, creative, and fully engaged citizens by investing in innovative ideas, convening interested parties, sharing learning, and advocating for change. Tides Canada Foundation is a pan-Canadian charity that works to build bridges among sectors and direct more philanthropy into solutions for social and environmental challenges.

Indigenous Rights

The enduring legacy of colonialism touches every facet of the lives and rights of Canada's Indigenous Peoples. Along with land claims and other traditional rights, the mobilization encompasses a range of essential issues in protecting the environment and combatting climate change, and a consistent defence of the popular right to challenge all levels of governments in the face of legal and political repression. The tragic and

---

4   These examples are illustrative only and do not reflect the wide range of activities by Canadian private and public foundations. Some idea of the diversity of these organizations can be found by examining the membership of Philanthropic Foundations of Canada (PFC) at https://pfc.ca/members/.

ongoing impacts of the physical and sexual torture of Indigenous children in residential schools is a major focus of advocacy. The tragedy of missing and murdered Indigenous women has also mobilized significant advocacy efforts by Indigenous groups and their allies.

Mobilization around all these complex and intertwined issues have brought advocacy for Indigenous rights to the forefront of political mobilization in Canada. The organizations that give voice to Indigenous concerns include nonprofits and federal, provincial and regional or local representative bodies, along with issue-specific coalitions and elected and traditional leaders. A special feature of Indigenous advocacy is the fact that various levels of Indigenous governments are involved in advocacy directed to the other levels of government in Canada, often with the same objectives as Indigenous nonprofits. As expressed by Trevor Tombe and Daniel Béland (2022):

> Our country is not run by a single government in Ottawa, nor by 13 provincial and territorial capitals. Instead, thousands of individual governments spanning multiple levels, including municipal and Indigenous ones — each with distinct responsibilities, authority, governance structures, financial resources and connections to Canadians — all play a role.

Examples of representative bodies advocating for Indigenous rights include the Assembly of First Nations, a gathering of Canadian First Nations as represented by their chiefs, and the Congress of Aboriginal Peoples, a national organization representing the large numbers of Indigenous Peoples who live off reserves, in either urban or rural areas across Canada. The Inuit Tapiriit Kanatami is a non-profit organization in Canada representing Inuit Peoples across Inuit Nunangat and the rest of Canada, with the mission of serving as a national voice protecting and advancing the rights and interests their peoples. The Métis National Council represents the democratically elected leaders of various Métis governments and represents their interests both in Canada and internationally. The Native Women's Association of Canada (NWAC) is a national organization representing the political voice of Indigenous women, girls, and gender-diverse people in Canada, inclusive of First Nations on and off reserve, status and non-status, disenfranchised, Métis, and Inuit (NWAC n.d.).

There are numerous regional associations representing Indigenous Peoples, including the Union of BC Indian Chiefs, the Southern Chiefs Organization in Manitoba, and the Grand Council of the Crees, operating in Quebec. In April 2022 the latter participated in establishing a Cree, Inuit, and Naskapi Forum of Northern Quebec (Grand Council of the Crees 2023).

Indigenous Nonprofits and Charities and Advocacy

As discussed earlier in this chapter, many Indigenous organizations are opposed to applying for charitable status, viewing it as a form of colonial control. For many others, however, the advantages of the status are attractive. John Lorinc (2019) reports that in Atlantic Canada, a growing number of First Nations are registered as qualified donees under federal income tax rules. Many Indigenous or Indigenous-focused nonprofits and charities, including those involved in social and family services, play a vital role in advocacy.

The Institute for the Advancement of Aboriginal Women is an Alberta-based non-profit organization that recognizes the role, value, and achievement of Aboriginal women in society and raises awareness about the challenges and obstacles they face (IAAW n.d.). Raven is a registered charity with a mission to raise funds for Indigenous Peoples' access to justice. Raven raises funds to support its core work of providing Indigenous Peoples with reliable, long-term support so they can defend their legal rights within a thriving natural habitat (Raven n.d.). Indspire is a national Indigenous registered charity that invests in the education of First Nations, Inuit, and Métis people for the long-term benefit of these individuals, their families and communities, and Canada (Indspire n.d.).

The First Nations Child and Family Caring Society is a national non-profit organization providing policy, education, and networking services to First Nations child and family service agencies in Canada. Its executive director, Cindy Blackstock, a member of the Gitxsan First Nation, has long played a leading role in advocacy for the rights of Indigenous children and families. In recent years she gave crucial leadership to successful negotiation with the federal government of an agreement-in-principle to settle a multi-billion-dollar lawsuit initiated by the Assembly of First Nations with respect to chronic underfunding of child welfare for First Nations and the physical, sexual, and mental abuse suffered by Indigenous children in the system. The agreement provided for $40 billion in compensation to survivors and for reform of the Indigenous child welfare system (Kochie 2022).

Allies and Alliances

Public understanding of the historical injustices suffered by Canada's Indigenous Peoples was greatly heightened by the publication in December 2015 of ninety-four recommendations contained in the report of the Truth and Reconciliation Commission, established to examine the history and legacy of the residential school system. But it was the identification by the Tk'emlúps te Secwépemc Nation (previously known as the Kamloops Indian Band) of the remains of about two hundred children who had been students at the Kamloops Residential School in May 2021 that inspired what appeared to be a major change in popular consciousness. This revelation initiated a period of reflection and mourning across the country. Flags on federal buildings were lowered to half-mast for five months, and international media followed the story closely (White 2022). More unmarked graves continued to be identified at residential schools across Canada over the next years, growing still further the sympathy and desire to act of non-profit supporters of Indigenous rights.

Examples include the Statement of Reconciliation issued by YMCA of Canada (2021) on Canada Day, July 1, 2021. Community Foundations of Canada (2021) also published a statement on reconciliation on that date. After the identification of unmarked graves at the former Kamloops Residential School, the ONN (2021) posted on ways that nonprofits could take action to support Indigenous communities.

Other nonprofits and charities have developed their support for Indigenous rights and for reconciliation over the last decade or more. In 2016, the Circle on Philanthropy and Aboriginal Peoples in Canada partnered with Philanthropic Foundations of Canada, Inspirit Foundation, Counselling Foundation of Canada, Martin Family Initiative, Lawson Foundation, J.W. McConnell Family Foundation, Ontario Trillium Foundation, Community Foundations of Canada, and Canadian Environmental Grantmakers' Network to create the Journey to Reconciliation Webinar Series (Lawson Foundation 2016).

The Gordon Foundation is a charity dedicated to protecting Canada's water and empowering Canada's North, which dedicates its resources to ensuring that public policy in Canada reflects its founders' values of independent thought, protecting the environment, and full participation of Indigenous Peoples in decision-making. Accordingly, the Foundation's projects involve collaboration and partnerships with various Indigenous organizations and individuals (Gordon Foundation. n.d.).

In Canada, Amnesty International and Greenpeace have both been active in support of Indigenous rights and reconciliation. Since 2004 Amnesty has developed its Stolen Sisters campaign to end discrimination and violence against Indigenous women in Canada (Amnesty International n.d.). Many of the campaigns of Greenpeace to protect the environment are carried out in explicit solidarity with Indigenous Peoples — such as the March 2018 participation in the march of ten thousand people to protect land, rivers, streams, and the Pacific Ocean from the potentially disastrous impact of the proposed Kinder Morgan pipeline (Firempong 2018).

Indigenous community mobilization and advocacy have a particularly profound impact on environmentalism in Canada. As reported by Ken Coates and JP Gladu (2023) in the *Globe and Mail*:

> The rise of Indigenous environmentalism is a profoundly important and largely quiet revolution. Indigenous communities speak for themselves on matters of protection, conservation and development. They accept ecological roles when and if opportunities arise, and they speak up when the system moves too slowly or inadequately. Non-indigenous groups, including industry, government and non-governmental organizations, have learned to listen and even to accept Indigenous direction.

Non-profit Advocacy Will Not Be Curtailed

Advocacy efforts are integral to the missions of nonprofits and essential for the sector to not only survive but flourish. Speaking as the executive director of FoodShare Toronto, Paul Taylor (2021) emphasized that nonprofits and charities could only make an impact if they pushed for political change.

Joanne Cave (2016) provides a compelling example of nonprofits continuing essential advocacy and research efforts in spite of government-imposed obstacles. The Native Women's Association of Canada, founded in 1974, is a registered non-profit organization with thirteen affiliated women's organizations across Canada. In 2005, NWAC initiated the ground-breaking Sisters in Spirit campaign, which culminated with the launch of a statistical database of 582 missing and murdered Indigenous women and girls across Canada. These efforts had a significant impact, providing essential resources to for policymakers, social justice organizations, and law enforcement officials across the country and for the inquiry on the issue, launched by Prime Minister Trudeau and his Cabinet in 2016.[5] NWAC persisted in this essential work, despite the Government of Canada redirecting NWAC's $10 million funding allocation in 2010, discontinuing its Sisters in Spirit database work. NWAC responded by working with two advocacy organizations (No More Silence and Families of Sisters in Spirit) to develop a database with data provided by victims' families. NWAC and its partners used grassroots organizing and community-led data collection to continue to highlight the ongoing tragedy of missing and murdered Indigenous women and girls.

This example demonstrates vividly that despite attempts to restrain or muzzle advocacy, this vital work continues. For non-profit charities the activities may take place through umbrella organizations, coalitions, or community engagement. For the rest of the sector, advocacy continues to develop in scope and through a variety of forms, including research and education, local and pan-Canadian mobilizations, and internet-based activities. Nonprofits keep advocating for community interests and social, economic and environmental justice, and will continue to do so because it is vital to their mission. This work provides an essential service not only for the communities and constituencies served by these nonprofits, but indeed for all Canadians.

---

5   Cave also notes the significant contributions of the Assembly of First Nations, the Native Youth Sexual Health Network, No More Silence, Families of Sisters in Spirit, and Amnesty Canada's No More Stolen Sisters initiative.

CHAPTER 5

2020: A Year of Turbulence

The year 2020 marked a turning point for nonprofits in Canada in important ways. With the onset of the COVID-19 pandemic, both the funding patterns and the service models were radically disrupted. The years 2020 and 2021 across North America also witnessed an explosion of struggle and solidarity efforts in opposition to anti-Black racism,[1] and in Canada to a dramatic rise in popular consciousness concerning Indigenous rights. A review of these events reveals a great deal about both the precarity and the resilience of the sector. It also provides important insights into the still-evolving forces shaping the future of nonprofits in Canada.

Impact of the Pandemic

Disruption of Services and Funding

Reporting for the *Globe and Mail* in 2020, Paul Waldie (2020) wrote: "The pandemic has hit charities on all fronts. The weakening economy has cut donations while government restrictions on social gatherings have ended fundraising events. And even as charities cut costs, they are being stretched further as demand for their service soars." Waldie also noted non-profit managers' observation that many nonprofits were barely hanging on and their fear that these agencies would go under when the federal government ended emergency support for wages and rent. Pamela Valentine, chief executive at the Multiple Sclerosis Society of Canada, stated that the non-profit she led had seen a $21 million drop in donations and laid off 165 people — nearly half its staff.

Also reported by Waldie were the following statistics gathered by Volunteer Canada, IPSOS and Volunteer Management Professionals

---

[1] Other examples of popular resistance were also evident during this period, including in opposition to anti-Asian racism and in resistance to right-wing anti-vaccination and masking protests, which culminated in the blockade of Parliament in downtown Ottawa in 2022.

of Canada: for non-profit agencies reporting in the first months of the pandemic, 29% had suspended, postponed, or cancelled all services, 67% some services, and only 4% none. On the other hand, only 2% had increased all their services, while 44% had increased or expanded some services, and 54% reported no increase or expansion. The researcher and public commentator Nik Nanos (2020) described the non-profit sector as an "unseen victim" of the pandemic, as many donations were on hold due to the economic uncertainty created and public health limitations restricted the ability of service providers to host events, deliver programs, and reach out to marginal groups.

Bruce MacDonald (Lasby 2020), president and CEO of Imagine Canada, wrote (seven weeks into lockdown) that charities across the country were responding to the pandemic by modifying existing programs, developing new ones, and implementing measures to help prevent the spread of the virus — all in dramatically changed working environments. He also noted:

> The pandemic is significantly damaging the financial and human health of our organizations. Charities across the sector are reporting revenues down markedly, with significant layoffs in progress — and more on the horizon. The size and scope of these shifts is beyond anything that we have seen before, far exceeding what we saw in the 2008/2009 financial downturn and with such broad effects even the most diversified revenue bases are seriously affected.

The pan-Canadian charity Volunteer Canada worked with Volunteer Management Professionals of Canada, as well as Spinktank and Ipsos, to survey their member agencies in the fall of 2020, with a focus on the impact of COVID on donations and employee community engagement. They concluded:

> The COVID-19 pandemic continues to have a profound impact on our health, the economy, and our social wellbeing, while illuminating the vulnerabilities and inequities in communities. This has placed enormous stress on the non-profit sector, as basic operations have been disrupted, resources have decreased, and the need for services has spiked. (Volunteer Canada et al. 2020)

From research and survey work done in collaboration with OCASI (Ontario Council of Agencies Serving Immigrants), John Shields, Valerie Preston and Jayesh D'Sousa (2023) reported that many community-based settlement organizations were under great threat during the first few months of the pandemic. These authors also observed that while there was a loss of donations and other revenues, for almost half of the organizations surveyed, they were not in a position to devote scarce resources for extra fundraising initiatives, especially given the bleak fundraising landscape at the time. This was a situation shared by the non-profit sector as a whole.

Based on surveys of their member organizations, the ONN, in collaboration with Assemblée de la Francophonie de l'Ontario (AFO), highlighted the serious negative impacts of the pandemic on community service organizations, as well as the failure of government, three months into the pandemic, to provide the vital aid necessary for non-profit agencies to survive. Responses to a bilingual survey by nearly 1,200 organizations revealed:

- $90 million in revenue losses among the 1,100 organizations that completed the survey
- 1 in 5 organizations expecting to close within six months
- 23% of nonprofits expecting their situation to get worse, including 40% of sports, recreation, and other social clubs and 31% of arts, culture and heritage organizations (ONN and AFO 2020).

Findings in these surveys were consistent across the non-profit sector from all types of organizations vital to Ontario and Canadian communities: health and social services, arts and culture, sports and recreation, faith groups, and environmental groups. Some non-profit organizations, however, were more negatively impacted than others. Arts and culture organizations, given their concentration of funding from sales and donations, were particularly negatively impacted by falling revenues and closure of activities during the pandemic.

Response by Funders

The pandemic created a situation for nonprofits which was clearly one of crisis, threatening the very survival of many service agencies and the essential services they provide. The sector responded with a concerted advocacy campaign outlining their difficult situation and the threats to the populations they serve, and demanding an appropriate government response.

Although a portion of non-profit organizations were able to access some important federal support oriented towards essential business continuity, such as the wage subsidy and rent relief programs, this was far from enough for the needs of the sector as a whole (Ireton 2021). Government aid programs were designed with private sector business in mind and hence lacked sensitivities to the specific circumstances of non-profit organizations. As summarized by Social Planning Toronto (SPT) from their viewpoint in Canada's largest municipality:

> The financial relief measures announced by the Federal government thus far meet only a fraction of the sector's needs, and the current eligibility criteria exclude many. This jeopardizes the services and supports Toronto communities need as we recover from this crisis. Adults and children experiencing poverty or food insecurity, vulnerable or marginalized youth, seniors, women facing domestic violence, people with disabilities, individuals with mental health challenges — entire populations across our city will suffer from decreased sector capacity. An investment in the sector is a critical investment in community and individual rehabilitation and reconnection. (SPT 2020)

In the same communique, Social Planning Toronto joined its voice to the pan-Canadian campaign initiated by Imagine Canada for a national grant program to help charities and nonprofits sustainably weather the challenges of COVID-19. Many other non-profit organizations took up similar themes, while also demanding vital support from provincial governments.

In a blog post highlighting the vital role nonprofits play for community members, Melanie Rodriguez (2020) outlined why nonprofits across Ontario, including the Health Charities Coalition, were joining the ONN in calling for the provincial government to create a stabilization fund for the non-profit sector:

> From isolation support programs for cancer patients to the doubling of phone service sessions for children experiencing mental health challenges, many non-profit services are needed now more than ever before. But increased demand and need

for organization services are not being met with increased funding. Close to three-quarters of nonprofits have seen decreased funding and one in five nonprofits have closed and may not reopen [others] are struggling to keep their doors open. (Rodriguez 2020)

The response of the federal and provincial governments was not proportional to the needs; nor was support distributed in an equitable manner among different types of nonprofits. Nevertheless, the aid that was provided played a major role in ensuring the survival of many community agencies and their essential services. As reported for Imagine Canada by David Lasby (2021),

> the only major area where revenues are on the rise is government funding, with two fifths of organizations reporting increases, largely driven by Federal and Provincial support programs. Federal government supports are playing a significant financial role, with 42% of charities applying for at least one program. The vast majority of organizations (86%) are in-scope for support and many have benefited. The Canada Emergency Wage Subsidy (CEWS) has the highest uptake (over half of charities with paid staff), followed by the Canada Emergency Business Account (CEBA). Larger organizations are more likely to have received supports, as are Health charities. Smaller charities and Philanthropic intermediaries are more likely to be out of scope for support programs, as are charities that primarily depend on earned income and gifts and donations.

Shields, Preston and D'Sousa (2023) analyzed the rapid and flexible support provided by the federal department of Immigration, Refugees and Citizenship Canada (IRCC) to maintain essential supports provided by community-based immigrant service agencies (ISAs):

> With the outbreak of the COVID-19 emergency, fortunately, IRCC moved quickly to stabilize immigrant-serving agencies. They shifted their operations to virtual mode declaring IRCC was "open for business." As the pandemic began, IRCC was in the middle of assessing 5-year settlement programing applications and with great effort, they completed the process in April

2020 and awarded some $4 billion in contracts. The contracts provided crucial future funding for ISAs.... Significantly, IRCC guaranteed existing funding amounts for agencies through the crisis and placed in abeyance their accountability expectations, with other governments following IRCC's lead.

In the case of immigrant settlement agencies, in order to preserve services and stabilize the settlement sector during the first two years of the pandemic, IRCC actually suspended many of its new public management (NPM) rules of funding and accountability governance to promote more sector collaboration and financial stability. There was a recognition by IRCC that NPM was a destabilizing force during the COVID-19 crisis. NPM was identified as impeding the viability and enhancing the precarity of non-profit based services and hence the move away from it. The question remains as to whether this approach was simply a short-term emergency-based reaction by the state to be followed by a restoration of NPM and austerity practices, or a case of lesson learned with a permanent diminishing of NPM approaches. The early evidence on the ground suggests that there is a graduated return to old practices informed by NPM by government post-pandemic (Preston et al. 2024).

Some federal support was also targeted for Indigenous Peoples during the pandemic. Kristy Kirkup (2020) reported $305 million provided in March 2020 through the Indigenous Community Support Fund, including $15 million to address the needs of Indigenous Peoples living in urban centres and off-reserve. Shortly afterwards, the latter amount was increased to $75 million.

Support from Foundations

In response to the impact of the pandemic on the non-profit sector, many private and public foundations across Canada worked to align their funding policies with rapidly changing priorities. In a special report published in April 2022, Imagine Canada examined various initiatives to make funding models more responsive, equitable, relevant, and effective. One important finding was that Philanthropic Foundations of Canada (PFC) had determined that through 2020, 56% of its member philanthropic agencies surveyed had removed restrictions on existing grants. This allowed the service organizations to use funds already received according to the most urgent needs — not necessarily the targeted activities originally negotiated with the funder (Imagine Canada 2022).

An example of the response of an individual foundation comes from Sandy Houston (2020a) of the Metcalf Foundation:

> Today I am writing to share news about a recent Metcalf Foundation Board decision. Like many of our philanthropic colleagues we will significantly increase the amount of money we will grant this year, contributing much needed additional resources to sustain the remarkable contributions of the non-profit sector. Our Board has approved $2 million in new funding and up to $1 million from our 2020 grants budget toward three strategies aimed at impacts of COVID-19: emergency response, sector-focused support, and forward-looking action. These funds are in addition to our existing grant programs and ongoing commitments....
>
> Unrestricted funding is more critical than ever for non-profit organizations. Emergency funds will be distributed to Metcalf grantees and long-time partners working in our program areas. Early funding priority will be given to our Performing Arts and Inclusive Local Economies programs, both of which have been particularly hard hit by the pandemic. Within this emergency envelope, we also intend to increase support for organizations working in our program areas that are led by and focus on equity-seeking communities, as we know they are disproportionately impacted by this crisis. We believe that a healthy and empowered non-profit sector is fundamental to our society. Sector-focused funding will support umbrella, network, and other sector-wide organizations who are delivering important services to the non-profit community. These organizations champion sector needs and issues, produce timely sector analysis, and are generating widely accessible resources to aid nonprofits in responding to COVID-19 and its ongoing impacts.

In a display of non-profit sector resilience, many charitable-based funders, like Metcalf, have responded to the needs of non-profit actors with additional grants and more flexible funding forms. Canadian foundations have recognized the critical position of non-profit organizations in addressing societal needs but also the precarious position of the non-profit sector, particularly in a crisis like the pandemic. The actions of foundations offer important sources of funding assistance to nonprofits to address emergency needs and they provide best practice models for other funders to learn from. However, it is also the case that foundations in Canada have a limited founding footprint, with about $8 billion in annual funding dollars as of 2021 (PFC 2022), although many of these funding dollars go to very large charities like hospitals.

Continuity of Services and the Role of Technology

In an update from Imagine Canada after year one of the pandemic, Lasby (2021) reported that the situation for nonprofits had improved somewhat, based on responses to the same questions that had been posed shortly after the onslaught of the pandemic:

- three-quarters of the agencies surveyed were operating with modified procedures, and the percentage forced to close had declined from 18% to 8%;
- having undertaken dramatic efforts to adapt to the challenges of remote work and new forms of service delivery, more agencies were feeling positive about their increasing organizational capacity; and
- demand for services was steadily increasing, and the problem of demand outstripping capacity was becoming more acute, particularly in the areas of education and health.

Reporting on the responses of community-based immigrant service agencies in Quebec and Ontario, Shields, Preston and D'Souza (2023) also noted that the situation for agencies had improved significantly. The two key factors they identified behind the improvement — other than a supportive response from the main government funders (IRCC in Ontario and the provincial government in Quebec), as previously discussed — were extensive and impressive efforts of collaboration both among the agencies and with public institutions, and a largely successful transition to online services.

In a December 2020 update on the impact of the pandemic on nonprofits, the Community Sector Council of Nova Scotia (now Impact Organizations of Nova Scotia) (2020, 15) also reported that partnerships and innovation had been key to the sector's re-establishment. Initiatives included strengthening existing links between organizations, establishing new ones, and twinning better-resourced agencies with those with less capacity. Improved communication and partnership with funders were also seen as key in the recovery process.

The transition to online rather than in-person services, along with the matching uptake in remote work by agency staff, was generally accomplished successfully, despite serious obstacles. Waldie (2020) tells of non-profit leaders reporting that years of relentless pressure by donors to cut costs had left their organizations without the technological resources needed to cope with the pandemic. He noted that despite the obstacles, statistics gathered by Volunteer Canada, IPSOS, and Volunteer Management Professionals of Canada showed the following at the end of 2020: 66% of reporting agencies had continued by transforming some of their services to virtual, and 12% had transformed entirely to virtual; 43% had continued by developing safe practices for in-person services while 16% had changed all their services in this manner. In the case of the non-profit immigrant service sector, during the height of the pandemic the federal government provided additional funding to support technology upgrades. Surveys of settlement organizations in Ontario and Quebec two years into COVID-19 revealed that, although under great strain, agencies and their workers were able to continue to provide high quality services matching pre-pandemic standards to their client groups and in many cases even expand their reach (Shields, Preston, and D'Souza 2022).

Debbie Douglas, executive director of the Ontario Council of Agencies Serving Immigrants (OCASI), described how, for community service organizations, including umbrella organizations like OCASI, the pandemic changed the issue of online services from one of choice to one of necessity. Previously OCASI had been operating with a mix of direct and online services, with some creative tensions among the staff about which should be primary:

> And then the COVID pandemic hit. All business stopped and within a two-day period we had pivoted completely to remote work with all programming moving online. Because we had invested in hardware and software over the years we were in good shape to accommodate most staff although we had to and are still purchasing laptops, etc. to ensure that staff have all the tools they need to continue to deliver quality work.

This allowed us to put our attention to the needs of the membership and the sector as whole. (Douglas 2020b)

The work of the Settlement Sector and Technology Task Group (managed by AMSSA, reporting to IRCC's National Settlement and Integration Council) provides an instructive example of community initiatives and collaboration in overcoming the service impacts of the pandemic, as well as vital support from the federal government to accomplish this. The group was convened with the goal of discovering, examining, and learning about the settlement sector's needs to successfully implement digital and hybrid service delivery. The mandate was to identify multiple digital transformation and hybrid service delivery models (where relevant), rather than aiming at one unique model that might not easily be replicable within the entire sector. The work included consideration of infrastructure, privacy issues including advice and protocols on safeguarding information, professional development for staff including digital literacy, and addressing the digital divide among newcomers and in their communities (Settlement Sector and Technology Task Group 2020).

Community-based immigrant service associations were consulted with a view to producing an overview of the current landscape of digital service provision and practices, gaps, challenges, risks, and opportunities for service providers. Attention was given to specific changes required to:

- support a digital transformation and a hybrid service delivery model, where relevant;
- provide insight into possible overlooked opportunities to support rural and remote placed newcomers via the use of LoFi technologies such as television/radio/telephone; and
- assess the potential of distance learning tools, welcoming packages, pen pal community connection projects, pre-arrival relationship building, etc. when digital delivery was not suitable for all clients or all services.

The final report, *From Silos to Solutions: Toward Sustainable and Equitable Hybrid Service Delivery in the Immigrant & Refugee-Serving Sector in Canada*, including recommendations, was completed in April 2021 (IOM 2021).

It is clear that coming out of the pandemic stage of COVID-19, the future of non-profit services will be that of hybrid service delivery. This development is significant because of the added infrastructure costs to already financially strained non-profit service providers, the flexibility it provides to clients (especially those in remote or under-serviced locations), and the possibility that it opens greater competition for clients between non-profit providers since it eliminates geographical barriers to service provision. This is a situation that greatly advantages larger non-profit providers with economies of scale over smaller local community providers, which may be forced to close.

Community service agencies also undertook many initiatives to provide basic economic assistance to vulnerable groups and to assist their own staff in accessing the government benefits available during the pandemic. For example, Social Planning Toronto (SPT) produced a website to help front-line workers navigate the financial and housing support programs. CovidHelpTO was designed to help front-line workers answer their clients' most basic questions around financial and housing supports and was made available in fourteen languages, as well as English (SPT 2020).

In similar initiatives, OCASI reported that their work to ensure various government income supports were reaching the most marginalized and those made most vulnerable by their economic situations and/or their identities had raised over a quarter of a million dollars. This was redistributed to Ontario residents who, due to their precarious immigration status or being undocumented, could not access government supports and had lost jobs in the underground labour market when the economy came to a standstill (Douglas 2020b).

Such initiatives demonstrate the innovative and resilient character of the non-profit sector that is brought to the fore through challenge and adversity. The struggle to fulfil nonprofits' social justice mission provides much of the fuel propelling organizations forward in difficult times. Marshalling civic spirit, fostering networks and collaborating toward good works is built into the DNA of the sector (Nakua 2023). However, to build back better, the non-profit sector needs capacity enhancements, including sustainable funding, spending flexibility, and technological investments. The precarious position of the non-profit sector was vividly revealed by the pandemic crisis. COVID-19 presented "a critical inflection point" for nonprofits (McKnight and Gouweloos 2021), where sector capacities have been tested and neoliberal approaches to the sector and society have been challenged.

Solidarity with Antiracist Struggles and Indigenous Rights

The COVID-19 pandemic has been both a great societal disrupter and a great revealer of structural inequalities, racism, sexism, and other repressions (Greenfield 2021; Lui 2021) that were allowed to deepen under neoliberal restructuring (Shields and Abu Alrob 2021, 138). The targeting of racial minorities, Indigenous Peoples and immigrants during COVID-19 has been labelled Coronaracism (International Monetary Fund 2020). Non-profit organizations representing and serving the highly vulnerable, including Black and Indigenous populations, have been among the most negatively affected by the pandemic since they are usually smaller, highly dependent on volunteers, and thinly resourced coming into the pandemic with especially precarious client populations (Ireton 2021). These populations were the most vulnerable to COVID-19 and more likely to fall through the cracks of pandemic supports offered by governments (Buckner 2020). The combination of years of neoliberal austerity, the pandemic, and systemic racism and marginalization was the equivalent to a "medical Katrina" (Davis 2020). However, the COVID-19 crisis did open up progressive challenges to racism and the divisive politics of neoliberalism (Allen and Yang 2020). Grassroots non-profit organizations based in oppressed communities organized during the pandemic and engaged in anti-racist and solidarity struggles. The situation also resulted in a process of critical self-reflection on the part of the non-profit sector itself.

In 2020, as the pandemic in Canada arrived in full force, there was already a rising public consciousness and widespread mobilization around Indigenous rights and anti-Black racism. As well as being active in the mobilization around these issues, the non-profit sector was also confronted with the challenges of internal transformation related to anti-racism and Indigenous reconciliation.

> On May 25, 2020, Minneapolis police officer Derek Chauvin murdered George Floyd. Protests ignited in Minneapolis and then spread quickly to cities across the United States and around the world, with estimates indicating that these were

the largest, most diverse and longest-lasting protests in North American history. (Ajadi and Thomson 2021)

The powerful wave of protest against the George Floyd murder and many other cases of anti-Black racism had a strong impact on Canadian nonprofits, many of which reacted quickly with clear expressions of solidarity. One powerful example of such declarations came from Amnesty International Canada (2020):

> The history, events and choices that led to the 8 minutes and 46 seconds it took on May 25 2020 for one police officer, aided and abetted by three of his fellow officers, to kill George Floyd, is a long complex one. While this tragedy occurred in the US and the context, scale and scope of anti-Black racism differs accordingly, we recognize and acknowledge that similar incidents have and continue to occur here and that Canada has its own underlying history of anti-Black racism. Reconciliation with that history must begin with truth, even if hearing it is painful. Racism and the systems that uphold it are, for the most part, very much out in the open. Equality does not live in a statement or a gesture. Reconciliation is not an event; it is a journey.

The statement also outlined the commitments made by Amnesty International Canada:

- continuing to work with grassroots allies and partners to better understand how and where the expertise, knowledge, and resources Amnesty International brings can add the most value and be welcomed;
- focusing its contribution to addressing anti-Black racism where organizations and individual partners with the greatest expertise and history of anti-Black racism work believe it can add value; and
- establishing an external reference group to advise it as it continues to develop goals and activities for the long term, grounded in tremendous respect for those who have been doing the hardest and most emotionally intensive work to expose and address racism in Canada for years or even decades.

The non-profit sector in Canada was also marked by a significant increase in public attention to Indigenous rights. As discussed in the previous chapter, in May 2021 the Tk'emlúps te Secwépemc announced finding, through the use of ground-penetrating radar, the remains of as many as 215 children around the former Kamloops Indian Residential School in British Columbia's interior (Dickson and Watson 2021). Since then, numerous other First Nations have also searched school sites in their territories, often with the same shocking and heartbreaking discoveries.

This was by no means the beginning of significant public attention in Canada to Indigenous rights. Indigenous communities, organizations and leaders had been fighting for their rights, including Treaty rights, ever since the beginning of European colonization. A critical contemporary marking in this struggle is the Truth and Reconciliation Commission of Canada, active in Canada from 2008 to 2015, organized by the parties of the Indian Residential Schools Settlement Agreement. In May 2015, the Commission published its ninety-four "Calls to Action." In May 2016 Canada officially adopted the United Nations Declaration on Rights of Indigenous Peoples, removing its objector status almost a decade after the declaration was adopted by the UN General Assembly. In addition, as documented in Chapter 4, many non-profit organizations, including several foundations, had already begun to focus a significant portion of their work on Indigenous rights and reconciliation.

The continuing revelations, however, of unmarked graves at Canada's residential schools has intensified critical public awareness and understanding of these issues. The facts gradually unveiled the role of these institutions in the imprisonment, sexual abuse, torture, and even murder of Indigenous children stolen from their families. Many Canadians for the first time came to understand the true horrors of settler colonialism and cultural genocide for Canada's Indigenous Peoples. This growing awareness has also greatly impacted non-profit organizations.

In Canada, most non-profit organizations linked their commitment to anti-racist action to solidarity with a broader concern for Indigenous rights. Metcalf Foundation was one such organization:

> The broad and deep social justice movements focused on anti-Black and anti-Indigenous racism and the underlying structural racism within many of our institutions and

organizations has provoked much needed scrutiny and reflection among those in positions of power and privilege. Our Board and staff are listening and learning, and we are shifting our work in response. Within our COVID-19 strategy, we expanded support for organizations who are led by and/or focus on equity-seeking communities, who we know have been disproportionately impacted by this crisis. These efforts were greatly strengthened by the advice and direction provided by a committee of Black, Indigenous and other arts leaders of colour who helped guide Metcalf emergency funds to arts organizations that have fallen outside the parameters of our work. There is much more to be done, and we will be developing and expanding our efforts across our programs in the coming year. (Houston 2020b)

The type of scrutiny and reflection mentioned above was widespread in the non-profit sector during this period and led many organizations to a new appreciation for the importance of actively promoting diversity in all aspects of their structures and programming. The Community Sector Council of Nova Scotia (2020, 19), for example, reported the following examples of the breadth of the initiatives of Council member agencies:

- Partnering to offer a Reconciliation focused event with Mi'kmaq and African Nova Scotian musicians and artists for a collaborative musical art performance
- Putting up Black History and Mi'kmaq posters in all our sites, and welcoming a new Mi'kmaq member to the Board of Directors
- Adopting a grass roots approach to improvement as an organization in addressing inequities, with a small group leading internal and external consultations
- Offering the organization's interns extensive diversity training and opportunities to discuss inclusion, interculturalism and structural racism that impacts African Nova Scotians and Indigenous people in our communities
- Staff participation in "A Learning Journey" put together by our local Diversity and Inclusion Committee, including painting a Black Lives Matter mural on the front of our building,

- participating in a march and Orange Shirt Day, and committing to continuing education
- As an organization made up mostly of people who immigrated to Canada, we take racism very seriously and will fight for the rights of all peoples
- The release of an organizational statement on Anti-Black racism in June 2020 was followed by the hiring of an Equity, Diversity & Inclusion Coordinator to improve EDI practices across all departments in our organization and ensure training and focus on these topics for staff and board.

In October 2022, Imagine Canada provided an overview of its progress to date as well as future plans to advance anti-racism and anti-oppression work within the organization. It emphasized the importance of such work being properly resourced and tracked for accountability. Above all, the work had to be embedded in human resources practices. Related initiatives included working with the Non-profit Federal Data Working Group to bring equity considerations to the government's collection of non-profit sector data and advocating for reforms to government grants to allow for better working conditions for the sector's diverse workforce. As well, the organization was offering free, bilingual resources on human resources issues to non-profit leaders, including a section on "Equity & Decent Work" developed in collaboration with the Ontario Nonprofit Network (ONN) (MacDonald 2022).

Imagine Canada in 2023 released a major report, *Shifting Power Dynamics: Equity, Diversity and Inclusion in the Non-profit Sector*, based on a survey of non-profit and voluntary organizations in Canada, outlining equity, diversity, and inclusion (EDI) practices in the sector. It found that there was much work to be done on EDI. A key finding of the report is that

> while most non-profit leaders support equity, diversity, and inclusion, far fewer pursue it with deep intentionality. Non-profit leaders widely support the principles of equity, diversity and inclusion, see their value, and believe they are acting in accordance with them. Most organizations are also taking at least some steps to put their beliefs into action. However, many do not appear to be deeply or enduringly committed to EDI. For instance, roughly two fifths of organizations have not

conducted any form of equity audit (i.e., reviewed any aspect of their operations through an equity lens). Similarly, while strong majorities of organizations highlight EDI principles in their policies and follow equity-enhancing recruitment practices to some degree, significantly fewer have stand-alone EDI policies and/or regularly evaluate the effectiveness of their recruitment practices. Small and mid-sized organizations and white-led organizations are the least likely to be intentional in their pursuit of EDI. (Barr, Pontbriand, and Lasby 2023)

The disruptions of the pandemic and revelations it helped bring to the fore, were critically important for placing issues of equity, racism, and colonialism centre stage within the Canadian non-profit world. In terms of non-profit service targeting and advocacy around these issues, as well as the need to address anti-racism, colonialism, and inclusion within their own organizations and to diversify their workforce, anti-racism and reconciliation with First Nations have become priorities.

Lessons Learned and Looking to the Future

The onslaught and continuation of the COVID-19 pandemic was a major challenge for the non-profit sector in Canada. Agencies providing essential health and social services were forced to rapidly transition to online services, with interrupted and/or reduced funding. Donations dropped sharply for numerous charities, including social, human, and health service providers. At the same time, the needs of vulnerable groups served by the sector, especially racialized communities, expanded rapidly as a consequence of the pandemic.

Despite the difficult situation, the non-profit sector came through significantly better than many of its leaders, as well as observers, had feared. An unknown number of organizations did not survive, and many were weakened for a protracted period in terms of funding and personnel. But the sector as a whole, and many of its component organizations, demonstrated dramatically the stubborn resilience that is one of its fundamental characteristics (Shields et al. 2024).

One of the important reasons for this success was a spirit of collaboration. Services agencies as well as community and private foundations joined together in effective advocacy efforts to secure necessary funding. There was also extensive collaboration between nonprofits to maintain essential services for the communities they served and to extend these services where necessary to the most vulnerable.

Another essential factor was the timely and flexible response of many funders, including governments, to not just maintain funding in drastically changed circumstances but also to provide the flexibility in rules and conditions that was essential in the new circumstances. Overall, the response of funders provided a clear demonstration that the cost-cutting logic and stifling administrative procedures of NPM were not an unquestionable gospel, as they had been portrayed for so long. The revision of these rules and their application, in fact, proved to be essential to the survival of the agencies and the well-being of those they served.

However, the pandemic also highlighted and intensified some basic problems in the sector that require further reflection and continuing attention. Foremost is the issue of funding. Will funders continue to modify their policies to match the realities of managing nonprofits and meet the changing needs of those they serve? Or will they see the easing of the pandemic and its associated restrictions as an opportunity to revert to the "command and control" models that stifle innovation in programming and choke administrative capacity? Many sector leaders are optimistic that funding policies will continue to evolve in a progressive direction — but nothing is certain at this stage.

A worrying sign comes from a 2022 Ontario non-profit sector report on the state of the non-profit sector that found that 74% of Ontario non-profit organizations witnessed an increase in service demand with strong projections of continued expansion in need, but at the same time less than half of the organizations in the sector experienced revenue increases, and many of the increases were due to time-limited emergency pandemic funding (ONN and AFO 2022, 2–4). A service demand versus capacity gap is widening in the non-profit sector. In fact, the 2023 ONN report proclaimed that the sector is at a tipping point and is "running on fumes." The legacy of "doing more for less" continues to be a reality for most non-profit providers.

Furthermore, the issues of economic insecurity and inequality brought into relief by the pandemic, despite the efforts of nonprofits and their funders to ameliorate the impact, are intensifying as the economic challenges of inflation and job insecurity spread in Canada. The greatest impact is on the very people served by the non-profit sector, and the trends remain stubbornly gendered and racialized. The incessant growth of food bank usage across Canada (Reimer 2021), which has continued to accelerate since the beginning of the pandemic, shows the pitfalls of economic "recovery" for Canada's most vulnerable.

Human resources issues will provide additional challenges for the non-profit sector. Many of its current leaders, if not already retiring, will do so within a few years. New and younger staff need to be recruited, with leadership training and transitioning in mind. But this challenge is particularly difficult given the prevalence in the sector of low salaries, limited opportunities for promotion, and insecure contract work — precarious work — that has been produced by the neoliberal funding regime.

The ongoing movements for solidarity with Canada's Indigenous Peoples and in opposition to racism represent significant challenges — and opportunities — for Canadians as a whole. For the non-profit community sector, these issues demand ongoing attention with regards to mission fulfillment, advocacy, and equity and diversity in organizational matters.

The future of the non-profit sector remains unclear in many important aspects. But whatever the issues and challenges, they will be met with the same kind of resilience, solidarity, and community that permitted these organizations to weather the worst of the pandemic. Yet the sector will still continue to experience the structural problems of precarity and serious capacity limitations that hinder its effectiveness and its ability to more fully contribute to building strong and sustainable communities.

CHAPTER 6

Future Challenges and Opportunities

As outlined in this volume, the non-profit sector is a substantial presence in the Canadian political economy landscape. The sector is large, diverse, and complex, with multiple dimensions composing its makeup. The sector plays key functions in society, including its mission-based services and its advocacy role, which enhances the voices of the marginalized and promotes democratic engagement. Nonprofits as community-centred organizations are vital for the health of civil society and community-led development and sustainability.

Complex and Contradictory Relationships

As we have seen, neoliberalism has had a major impact on the non-profit sector. Neoliberal policymakers have worked to use non-profit organizations as part of their restructuring efforts. This has raised the issue of whether significant elements of the non-profit sector have been compromised toward meeting the goals of a neoliberal agenda over their social justice missions.

Some scholars view the non-profit sector under neoliberalism as part of a "shadow state" (Wolch 1990). The argument is that, as the neoliberal state moves along a path of withdrawing from many social welfare supports and restructures other supports along more austere and regressive lines, the non-profit sector is forced to take on the social welfare role. This has created a weaker and more precarious protective layer than previously existed. Some services are funded by governments by contracting with non-profit organizations under new public management principles. This is believed to result in state capture of contracted non-profit organizations, as they become financially dependent on the state funder and their operations directed through strict accountability measures by the neoliberal state. Even non-profit service providers not under state control through contract financing are drawn into this system by coming to play a safety valve role. In the words of Joan Roelofs (1995), the "Third Sector acts as a protective layer for capitalism." Nonprofits fill service gaps left by the retreating state as much as they can. In essence, according to this view, the non-profit sector enables an even deeper dismantling of the welfare state, with the non-profit sector becoming a de facto shadow state in service to neoliberalism (Singh Kelsall, Palmour, Marck, et. al 2023). This process subverts the social justice missions of the non-profit sector and undermines community cohesion, as the non-profit sector's dominant role becomes its use by neoliberalism to shrink the state and enhance the dominance of capitalist markets in society. The progressive potential of the non-profit sector, hence, comes to be neutralized (Milligan and Fyfe 2005; Kivel 2017).

The "shadow state" argument is compelling and identifies the reality of how the neoliberal state has made use of the non-profit sector as third-sector delivery agents, enforcing NPM accountability to state funders, and as bodies that carry the burden of neoliberal downloading. However, this one-dimensional and instrumental depiction of the sector fails to recognize that the relationship between the neoliberal state and the non-profit sector is actually a dynamic one, with contradictory regressive and progressive crosscutting currents. The "shadow state" outlook reveals the negative impacts of neoliberalism on nonprofits and community, but it neglects the social justice work and the community-building initiatives in which the sector is daily engaged. The non-profit sector as well often plays a mediator role (DeVerteuil, Power, and Trudeau 2020), providing a bridge between vulnerable communities and neoliberal governments, thereby mitigating the impacts of neoliberalism. What stands out is the centrality of the non-profit sector within contemporary neoliberal society.

The challenge for the sector is how to resist the most negative consequences of neoliberalism as many non-profit organizations need to continue to accept program funding from the neoliberal state for essential client services, and while the sector as a whole plugs holes left by a retreating state. This is the dilemma and debate that most visibly confronts food banks (Cressell Riol and Connelly 2023). Food banks play a major role in helping to address the worst effects of food insecurity, providing a critical service for those most in need. But in so doing they relieve pressure on the neoliberal state to address this crisis. In pursuit of their social justice mission, non-profit food banks are caught in a contradictory dynamic. In doing good work food banks may also help perpetuate the neoliberal agenda. As organizations that are grounded in communities to deal with the everyday reality of human needs, they by nature are pressed into action to address the immediate food crises facing individuals and families. Like food banks, the non-profit sector as a whole is positioned to offer a measure of protection that for many can mean the ability to survive or not. The non-profit sector also provides "spaces of citizenship by tolerating and sustaining those excluded by neoliberalism" (DeVerteuil 2017, 1520). Nonprofits create spaces of hope where vulnerable populations can find support and advocates that enable the voices of the dispossessed. In such ways the non-profit sector, as Geoffrey DeVerteuil (2017, 1520) notes, offers an "important cushioning and buffering that counter the excesses of the market and the [neoliberal] state, thwarting the unlimited power of both."

In some measure the contradictory currents found in the non-profit sector are reflected in the dynamics of resilience and precarity that the sector is forced to manage. The precariousness of nonprofits, as described in this volume, is fostered by neoliberal policy and societal restructuring; but sector resilience is in part motivated by non-profit social justice instincts and initiatives. It is in the advocacy role that nonprofits can best address this contradiction: to advocate for radical reform and help organize and amplify the voices of vulnerable communities — while at the same time providing practical services and relief.

While the non-profit sector may embody a contradictory set of relationships, it is important to note that the values embodied within many of its organizations reflect the aims of rebuilding society along pathways towards a more community-centred and egalitarian order. These include values of cooperation, sharing, service to the community, altruism, mutuality, reciprocity, solidarity, social justice, and amplifying voices of the vulnerable, minorities, and the unheard. While the non-profit sector as a whole cannot be viewed as a revolutionary institutional force, many of the values it upholds are transformative. Social movements linked to the sector, like Black Lives Matter and Idle No More, represent transformative voices and mobilizations for change. In this regard the non-profit sector constitutes a critical space for the preservation and nurturing of progressive ideas and movements. Of course, not all values found in the sector are progressive as there is also a history and presence of paternalism, colonialism, charity over empowerment, philanthrocapitalism (McGoey 2015), and strong anti-statism in some strains of communitarian thought. Also, neoliberal governments have used (or misused) ideas of voluntarism, "community responsibility," and "Victorian values" of "selflessness and benefaction" as ways of shifting responsibility for social support away from the state and onto individuals, families, neighbourhoods, and civil society (Hughes and Ketola 2021, 14–15).

The COVID-19 pandemic offers a useful case study of the shifting dynamics that have begun to challenge the hegemony of neoliberalism. In the post-pandemic world, the Canadian non-profit sector faces many challenges, but it is also a sector that is positioned to be part of the forces for progressive transformation. During the COVID-19 crisis there was a promise conveyed to "build back better" along with many grassroots movements, like Black Lives Matter and Indigenous mobilizations, that challenge the status quo. The pandemic brought to the fore the reality of shared risks and the necessity of societal sacrifice for collective benefit. Neoliberal notions of a limited and shrinking government during the crisis were set aside, and the state was "brought back in" with implementation of widespread social and health policies and programming. The primacy of deficit control was put aside during the pandemic in order to address pressing human needs. A conjunctural moment was opened where other priorities and policy perspectives in opposition to neoliberalism were available — where pandemic dynamics opened up progressive policy opportunities.

The neoliberal face of capitalism, of course, has proven itself to be a resilient force, adapting in the face of numerous crises in the past, as in the case of the 2009 financial crisis (Peck and Theodore 2019). Once again neoliberal political forces have advanced arguments post-pandemic in favour of funding restraint and deficit control, pushing against more progressive political winds. The headline of a 2022 Imagine Canada article captures the impact of such a direction for the non-profit sector: "Charities and Nonprofits Forced to Adapt as Debt and Deficit Reduction becomes Fiscal Priority" (Hillel 2022). The adoption of government austerity would reduce state funding to the sector while increasing societal demand for sector services and supports at a time when non-profit organizations' capacities have been severely strained. Keeping open a progressive policy window and strongly resisting a return to a neoliberal policy agenda is a key priority for the sector moving forward.

Into the Future

Going forward there are a number of issues and trends that are worthy of note for the non-profit sector. To begin, the dynamic tension between resilience and precarity, as discussed in this volume, will persist and the capacity of non-profit organizations to manage this fault line will continue to be tested, placing increased strain on the sector.

Speaking for the Sector

The issue of how to amplify the voice of the non-profit sector to enhance its effectiveness in society and on public policy is critical. The development of pan-Canadian organizations like Imagine Canada as a national voice and an important research and information resource for the sector has been positive. Imagine Canada helps to provide a larger profile and stronger media presence for non-profit issues. However, given the incredible diversity of the sector, the locally based character of most non-profit organizations, and the federalist political structure of Canada, the primary locus of action for nonprofits very often does not rest at the national level, as was made evident during the Voluntary Sector Initiative. Some of the most active non-profit advocacy takes place at the provincial level, undertaken by umbrella non-profit organizations and provincially based organizations like the Ontario Nonprofit Network. These organizations are closer to many grassroots issues facing nonprofits at the local and regional levels, where responsibility for most social, health, housing, and labour rest. The diversity of the sector means that, realistically, the expression of multiple voices from the sector will continue to be an essential need.

To express Indigenous, racial minority, and many other interests, organizations rooted in these specific groups need their own voice. What is required is for all these voices to be amplified. In this regard, non-profit organizations and funders need to prioritize the advocacy role of nonprofits and fund this activity. The advocacy role of nonprofits needs to be as important as their service function. Given the multiple voices in the sector, organizations need to improve their ability to work together and coordinate their advocacy efforts.

A related issue has been the proposal, directed initially at the federal level, for creating a so-called "home in government" for the non-profit/charitable sector. The Special Senate Committee on the Charitable Sector in its June 2019 report (Special Senate Committee on the Charitable Sector 2019) recommended that the federal government designate a minister for the sector, hire dedicated staff in the Privy Council Office, and appoint a deputy or associate deputy minister responsible for the sector. Support for this has been endorsed and promoted by organizations like Imagine Canada and the ONN. It is believed that having a dedicated minister and resources in government that are responsible for paying attention to the sector would be beneficial in bringing sector issues to the Cabinet table and increasing awareness of the sector and its contributions to society inside government (Schaper 2019). This reform of government structure could also be adopted at other jurisdictional levels in Canada.

While there are clearly advantages for increasing awareness of the non-profit sector and issues related to it within government, such measures would not constitute a significant power shift. Such a ministerial responsibility would likely be considered a minor portfolio within the structures of Cabinet and the state bureaucracy. The level of voice amplification for the non-profit sector, in all likelihood, would be modest. So, while it is an initiative worthy of support, this reform would unlikely be a "game changer" for the sector.

The Non-profit Sector Data Deficit

The lack of adequate statistical data on the non-profit sector (see Chapter 2) is a continuing problem that negatively impacts our knowledge of the sector and assessments of the sector's contributions to the economy and society. Even though the non-profit sector has a larger economic impact than many other sectors of society (like the agricultural sector and the transportation sector), regular reliable data on nonprofits is not collected by state statistical authorities (Barr 2021). Hence, we have only rough estimates of the sector's size and social and economic presence. This situation hinders a proper appreciation of the non-profit sector. This data deficit also has disruptive effects on service planning and community-based needs assessments. Cathy Barr (2021) observes:

> Lack of data on the number, location, activities, and impact of non-profit organizations makes it difficult for individual donors to make donation decisions and for governments and other institutional funders to allocate funding efficiently or

effectively. Lack of knowledge about how to locate, collect, link, analyze, and communicate data hinders nonprofits every day: in their ability to deliver programs and services, advocate for change, obtain and deploy funding, plan for workforce needs, demonstrate their impact, or make strategic decisions about virtually any aspect of their operations.

In a world where "measurable impact" and "return on investments" are the standards used in assessments of worth, lack of basic reliable data constitutes a significant disadvantage for the non-profit sector. What gets counted gets recognized and is better positioned for receiving funding. So-called evidence-based policymaking and funding models demand statistical data measures.

It is important to remain critical about over reliance on "hard" statistically driven approaches to assessments, as they often reinforce the status quo and play to neoliberal "measurement for success" paradigms. But there are also progressive uses for statistical data, which can be leveraged to educate and advocate about issues. "Factually" outlining the dimensions of policy problems like food insecurity, the housing crisis, racial exclusion, and Indigenous colonization can be effective social justice tools supporting non-profit services and advocacy demands.

It is also the case, however, that there are other ways of knowing, as Indigenous methodologies make clear (Kovack 2021; Bérard 2021). Qualitative-based assessments and "data" collections that tap into the everyday lived experiences of vulnerable populations, struggling communities, and nonprofits' activities remain essential for non-profit organizations. By capturing grounded realities, qualitative approaches add an invaluable, textured understanding to community needs and the lived experiences of exclusion and exploitation. Such approaches can extend beyond the use of focus groups and interviews into the employment of storytelling, for example (Intiar and Mbũrũ 2023). These kinds of experiences and needs are not always captured by statistical data collection.

Funding Is the Elephant in the Room

As discussed in Chapter 3, the funding of organizations in the non-profit sector remains a major subject of controversy. The financial health of nonprofits is vital for their ability to effectively provide services and perform advocacy/voice roles in society. In particular, government contract funding, as we discussed, is a focus of sector attention. The sentiment about funding concerns is well expressed in the following account:

> Recovering from the pandemic while also confronting new challenges is stretching the sector thin and antiquated funding models are failing. Over and over again, the sector has critiqued short-term and program-specific funding as they do not cover general operating costs necessary for nonprofits to deliver their programs and services.... Flexible and targeted funding is crucial to organizations' ability to respond quickly to a changing environment and deploy resources accordingly. The need for flexibility is especially important now during periods of rapid change. (ONN and AFO 2022, 11)

Clearly the necessity for funding reform is a key part of addressing problems confronting the non-profit sector. Without fundamental reform on this issue, it will be impossible for the sector to effectively address societal needs.

Post-pandemic Stresses

Post-pandemic, the non-profit sector has been confronted with a number of formidable challenges (Shields et al. 2024). These include a human resources crisis. As the labour force ages and demand for workers increases, employers have been scrambling to fill vacancies at all skill levels. The non-profit sector finds itself in a particularly vulnerable position in this regard, as its levels of pay and benefits are considerably lower than in both the public and for-profit sectors. As Yvonne Rodney (2023a) notes: "Even though non-profit workers are more highly educated than those in the broader economy, those working in the community-based agencies earn an average salary of $38,716 compared to $57,137 economy wide." Workers are in a better position today to demand fairer compensation, but financially strapped non-profit organizations are in a poor position to meet such expectations. Hence there is a growing number of job vacancies that organizations are not able to fill. Adding to this situation has been the reconsideration of work-life balance, as well as pandemic burnout for sector workers. This has resulted in the so-called "great reshuffle," as workers shift work priorities, retire, and leave the labour market (Rodney 2023a).

This is a situation that has particularly affected the ability of non-profit organizations to recruit and retain more highly skilled staff, such as IT specialists. As well, in terms of executive directors and senior managers, there has been a considerable number of retirements post-pandemic. These positions have been difficult to fill with qualified and experienced replacements. Replacement of such personnel has been further complicated as most nonprofits are flat organizations, with limited ladders of opportunity for renewal at this level.

The human resources crisis extends to volunteers. Volunteering has failed to return to pre-pandemic levels, with older volunteers particularly reluctant (for safety reasons among others) to re-engage. Younger cohorts have different volunteering patterns and are not making up the difference for the loss of senior volunteers (Rodney 2023b). For a sector that is heavily reliant on volunteers, filling these gaps places more work on an already stretched paid staff and further intensifies the grave labour challenges in the non-profit sector.

Another post-pandemic issue for non-profit organizations has been the negative impact of high inflation levels, which topped 8% in 2022. While there has been some moderation in rates since then, the cost implications for organizations already struggling with underfunding have been significant. Funders, particularly government ones, have not adjusted their funding formulas to address these added costs for non-profit organizations, further devaluing the already-limited dollars. This situation is creating another significant pressure on the capacity of the sector (Jensen 2023).

Financial pressures caused by the economic fallout from the pandemic have resulted in additional pressure due to declining donations to charities. While there has been some recovery in donation levels since the end of the pandemic, giving patterns have been impacted, with larger non-profit organizations receiving appreciably larger shares of donated dollars and an overall lower proportion of the population making donations to charity (likely due to their own weaker financial circumstances). Particularly for small and medium-sized nonprofits, this shift in donation patterns is resulting in an additional layer of financial insecurity (Barr and Jensen 2023).

Increased Service Demands and Sector Capacity

Demand for non-profit services has continued to expand. Cutbacks in government-provided services, resulting from neoliberal austerity and growing societal divides between haves and have nots, have placed expanding pressures on nonprofits to fill service gaps. Post-pandemic there has been a significant jump in the use of non-profit services, with demand exceeding the ability of the sector to deliver and limitations on both financial and human resources. In 2023 fully 57% of charities reported not being able to meet current demand (CanadaHelps 2023). And the service demands on nonprofits will continue to grow. Pre-pandemic, Imagine Canada (2018b) reported, as noted in Chapter 3, that by 2026 Canada will face a "social deficit" of $25 billion, with the expectation that non-profit organizations will meet these service demands. The social deficit has inevitably expanded in size given deepening societal polarization. The expectation by the neoliberal state that communities and the non-profit sector will be able to address these growing needs, as the social responsibilities of the state continue to shrink, is particularly unrealistic given the already overtaxed capacity of the sector. At the same time for-profit service providers continue to fight for an ever-growing share of service provision — and boosted profits — in sectors such as childcare and health. When the dramatic pan-Canadian expansion of childcare initiated by the federal government was completed with Ontario's signing on in 2022, this represented a significant expansion of non-profit services, as well as the non-profit labour force. However, for-profit childcare providers remain significant players in the game and continue to lobby for an even greater role. The *Globe and Mail* reported in 2023 that, according to an independent report by Isobel Mackenzie, BC's independent senior's advocate, the for-profit operators who provide more than half of the province's long-term care beds provided significantly less services than they were paid to deliver, while the non-profit providers supplied more services than their contracts funded (Hunter 2023). Clearly the non-profit sector is not capable of replacing the social welfare role of the state, and at best can only offer partial relief.

Conclusion

Nonprofits, as we have documented in this volume, are faced with many challenges. But out of adversity emerges inventiveness and resilience, and the sector has repeatedly proven its ability to rise to challenges. The precariousness found in the sector, however, has acted as an impediment to even stronger sector contributions to the broader community and poses a formidable threat to the ongoing capacity of the non-profit sector to adequately support communities.

Nonetheless, non-profit organizations continue to provide spaces for democratic dialogue and community-building, facilitate social justice mobilizations, and provide a wide range of essential health and social services, particularly to the most vulnerable in society. Nonprofits are bearers of values that provide alternatives to the excesses of marketization and neoliberal policies. It is a sector under stress but one that remains vital to society and to the preservation of healthy communities. Consequently, it is very important that there is a greater recognition and understanding of the non-profit sector's complex but overwhelmingly positive place in Canadian society.

Bibliography

Ajadi, Tari, and Debra Thompson. 2021. "The Two Pandemics of Anti-Black Racism and COVID-19 Are Tied Together." Special to the *Globe and Mail,* May 22.

Alexander, C., and S. Gulati. 2013. "An Economist's Case for Volunteering." TD Economics Opinion, April 23.

Allen, K., and J. Yang. 2020. "Twin Crises Spur Calls to Treat Racism as Public Health Crisis." *Toronto Star,* June 8: A1, A10.

Alonzi, Alta. n.d. "What Is the Difference? Project vs Program." Proposals for NGOs. proposalsforngos.com/whats-the-difference-project-vs-program/#google_vignette.

Amnesty International Canada. 2020. *Black Lives Matter: Amnesty Canada (ES) Statement on Anti-Black Racism.* August 17. amnesty.ca/human-rights-news/black-lives-matter-amnesty-canada-es-statement-on-anti-black-racism/.

Amnesty International. n.d. *No More Stolen Sisters.* amnesty.ca/what-we-do/no-more-stolen-sisters/.

Angelou, Maya. 2022. *Canadian Charities — How to Choose Which to Donate To, and Why.* Canadian Feed the Children, October 31. canadianfeedthechildren.ca/the-feed/canadian-charities/.

Ascoli, Ugo, and Costanzo Ranci. 2002. "The Context of New Social Policies in Europe." In *Dilemmas of the Welfare Mix: The New Structures of Welfare in an Era of Privatization,* edited by Ugo Ascoli and Costanzo Ranci. 1–24. New York: Kluwer Academic/Plenum Publishers.

Aucoin, Peter. 2005. "Decision-Making in Government: The Role of Program Evaluation." (Discussion Paper). Treasury Board of Canada Secretariat.

Baines, D., J. Campey, I. Cunningham and J. Shields. 2014. "Not Profiting from Precarity: The Work of Non-profit Service Delivery and the Creation of Precariousness." *Just Labour: A Canadian Journal of Work and Society* 22.

Barr, Cathy. 2021. "The Non-profit Sector's Ongoing Data Deficit." *The Philanthropist Journal,* May 4. thephilanthropist.ca/2021/05/the-non-profit-sectors-ongoing-data-deficit/.

Barr, Cathy, and Emily Jensen. 2023. *What Trends Will Impact Charities and Nonprofits in the Second Quarter of 2023?* Imagine Canada, April 27. imaginecanada.ca/en/360/what-trends-will-impact-charities-and-nonprofits-second-quarter-2023.

Barr, Cathy, Émilie Pontbriand, and David Lasby. 2023. *New Study on Equity, Diversity and Inclusion a Wakeup Call for White Led Organizations.* Imagine Canada, July 6. imaginecanada.ca/en/360/new-study-equity-diversity-and-inclusion-wake-up-call-white-led-nonprofit-organizations.

Beck, Ulrich. 1992. *Risk Society: Towards a New Modernity.* London: Sage Publications.

Beeby, D. 2014. "Canadian Charities Feel 'Chill' as Tax Audits Widen into Political Activities." *Toronto Star,* July 10. thestar.com/news/canada/canadian-charities-feel-chill-as-tax-audits-widen-into-political-activities/article_b58dd2d1-0d80-5dea-a3a0-fc3305196979.html.

Bérard, Diane. 2021. "Shelley Price: Storytelling the Philanthropic Landscape — Collective Restorying of Giving and Sharing Through Indigenous Perspectives." *The Philanthropist Journal,* June 8. thephilanthropist.ca/2021/06/shelley-price-storytelling-the-philanthropic-landscape-collective-restorying-of-giving-and-sharing-through-indigenous-perspectives/.

Broadbent, Ed. 1999. "Building on Strength: Improving Governance and Accountability in Canada's Voluntary Sector." Ottawa: Panel on Accountability and Governance in the Voluntary Sector. https://sectorsource.ca/resource/file/building-strength-improving-governance-and-accountability-canadas-voluntary-sector.

Brock, Kathy L. 2004. "Judging the VSI: Reflections on the Relationship Between the Federal Government and the Voluntary Sector." *The Philanthropist Journal,* October 1. thephilanthropist.ca/2004/10/judging-the-vsi-reflections-on-the-relationship-between-the-federal-government-and-the-voluntary-sector/.

Brown, L.A. 2021. "What Charities Wish You Understood about Fundraising." *Good Times,* February 23. goodtimes.ca/what-charities-wish-you-knew-about-fundraising/.

Buckner, Dianne. 2020. "For Some Nonprofits, COVID-19 Isn't Just a Struggle. It's a Do-or-Die Moment." *CBC News,* June 26.

Burgis, Ben. 2022. "Effective Altruism Is No Substitute for a Better Society." *Jacobin,* 47: 120–122 (Fall).

Burke, Mike, Colin Mooers and John Shields. 2000. "Critical Perspectives on Canadian Public Policy." In *Restructuring and Resistance: Canadian Public Policy in an Age of Global Capitalism,* edited by Mike Burke, Colin Mooers and John Shields. 11–23. Halifax: Fernwood Publishing.

Burrowes, A., and R. Laforest. 2017. "Advocates Anonymous: A Study of Advocacy Coalitions in Ontario." In *The Shifting Terrain: Non-profit Policy Advocacy in Canada,* edited by N.J. Mulé, and G.C. Desantis. 63–81. Montreal and Kingston – London – Chicago: McGill-Queens University Press.

CAF (Charities Aid Foundation) Canada. 2019. *Canada Giving 2019.* March. cafcanada.ca/wp-content/uploads/2019/03/CAF-Canada-Giving-US-FinalMASTER5.pdf.

Cameron, John D., and Olivia Kwiecien. 2019. "Advocacy, Charity and Struggles for Global Justice in Canada." *Canadian Journal of Development Studies* 40, 3: 330–347.

CanadaHelps. 2021a. *Why Canada Helps.* canadahelps.org/en/why-canadahelps/.

___. 2021b. *The Giving Report 2021.* canadahelps.org/en/the-giving-report/.

___. 2021c. *5 Reasons Why You Should Donate to Charity.* canadahelps.org/en/giving-life/giving-strategy/5-reasons-why-you-should-donate-to-charity/?-medium=FPMX&gad_source=1&gclid=CjwKCAiAjfyqBhAsEiwA-UdzJK-OG26V1uaEV6bMLSx_52x9F1YWjTwE6-0o-q1eXNx1dNNLEJSUEqxoC-QfIQAvD_BwE&gclsrc=aw.ds.

___. 2023. *The Greatest Challenges Facing Charities: This Year's Giving Report from CanadaHelps.* Charity Village, June 1. canadahelps.org/en/the-giving-report/download-the-report/.

Canadian Centre for Philanthropy. 2003. *The Capacity to Serve: A Qualitative Study of the Challenges Facing Canada's Non-profit and Voluntary Organizations (Summary)*. yumpu.com/en/document/view/51176027/the-capacity-to-servepdf-imagine-canada.

Cappe, Mel. 1999. "Building a New Relationship with the Voluntary Sector." Speech to the Third Canadian Leaders' Forum on the Voluntary Sector. Association of Professional Executives, Ottawa, May 31. epe.lac-bac.gc.ca/100/205/301/pco-bcp/website/06-07-27/www.pco-bcp.gc.ca/default.asp@language=e&page=clerksspeechesmessages&sub=clerksspeeches&doc=1999_volontary_e.htm.

Cave, Joanne. 2016. "The Changing Landscape for Non-profit Policy Advocacy." *The Philanthropist*, February.

Chambon, Adrienne, and Ted Richmond. 2000a. "Defining and Measuring Settlement Services: State of the Art and Current Debates." Presentation to the Annual Conference of the Canadian Evaluation Society.

___. 2000b. "L'évaluation des services d'établissement pour les personnes immigrantes et réfugiées: enjeux conceptuels et méthodologiques." *Cahiers de recherche sociologique*, 35: 167–183. L'évaluation sociale: un enjeu politique.

Chantier de l'économie sociale. 2020. "Découvrez l'économie sociale." chantier.qc.ca/.

Clutterbuck, Peter. 2019. "Evidence." *Catalyst for Change: A Roadmap to a Stronger Charitable Sector*. Report of the Special Senate Committee on the Charitable Sector. https://sencanada.ca/en/Content/SEN/Committee/421/cssb/54630-e.

Coates, Ken, and JP Gladu. 2023. "Slowly but Surely, Indigenous Peoples Are Gaining Control of Traditional Lands." *Globe and Mail*, March 3. theglobeandmail.com/opinion/article-slowly-but-surely-indigenous-peoples-are-gaining-control-of/.

Community Foundations of Canada. 2018. "What Is a Community Foundation?" communityfoundations.ca/wp-content/uploads/2019/05/What-is-a-Community-Foundation-english.pdf.

___. 2021. "Community Foundations of Canada Statement of July 1." communityfoundations.ca/july-1/.

Coule, Trace M., Jennifer Dodge and Angela M. Eikenberry. 2022. "Toward a Critical Non-profit Studies: A Literature Review." *Non-profit and Voluntary Sector Quarterly*, 51, 3: 478–506.

Craig, A., and S. Gulati. 2012. "An Economist's Case for Volunteering." TD Economics Opinion. td.com/document/PDF/economics/special/AnEconomistsCaseForVolunteering.pdf.

Cressell Riol, Katherine S., and Sean Connelly. 2023. "Beyond a Neoliberal Critique of Hunger: A Genealogy of Food Charity in Aotearoa New Zealand." *Agriculture and Human Values*, March 15. https://pubmed.ncbi.nlm.nih.gov/37359833/.

Community Sector Council of Nova Scotia (now Impact Organizations of Nova Scotia). 2020. "COVID-19 Impact on the Nova Scotia Non-profit and Voluntary Sector." December. https://ions.ca/wp-content/uploads/2020/12/COVID-19-Survey-2-Report-Final.pdfnovascotia.ca/nonprofitsector/documents/COVID-19-IMACT-REPORT.pdf.

Davis, Mike. 2020. "The Monster Enters." *New Left Review*, 122. https://newleftreview.org/issues/ii122/articles/mike-davis-in-a-plague-year.

DeVerteuil, Geoffrey. 2017. "Post-Welfare City at the Margins: Immigrant Precarity and the Mediating Third Sector in London." *Urban Geography*, 38, 10: 1517–1533. doi.org/10.1080/02723638.2017.1286840.

DeVerteuil, Geoffrey, Andrew Power, and Dan Trudeau. 2020. "The Relational Geographies of the Voluntary Sector: Disentangling the Ballast of Strangers." *Progress in Human Geography,* 44, 5: 919–937.

Dickson, Courtney, and Bridgette Watson. 2021. "Remains of 215 Children Found Buried at Former B.C. Residential School, First Nation Says." CBC News, May 29.

Douglas, Debbie. 2020a. "In the Field Newsletter Volume #99." OCASI. ocasi.org/field-newsletter-volume-99.

———. 2020b. "Hell No — We Ain't Going Back." Executive Director's Message. OCASI *In The Field,* September. ocasi.org/hell-no-%E2%80%93-we-ain%E2%80%99t-going-back

Draaisma, Muriel. 2022. "Charities in Canada Stretched Thin as Donations Drop, Demand Rises, Report Says." CBC News, April 5. cbc.ca/news/canada/toronto/canadian-charities-unprecedented-strain-giving-report-2022-1.6408393.

Eakin, Lyyn. 2002. *Supporting Organizational Infrastructure in the Voluntary Sector.* Ottawa: Voluntary Sector Initiative Sectretariat.

———. 2007. We Can't Afford to Do Business This Way: A Study of the Administrative Burden Resulting from Funder Accountability and Compliance Practices. Toronto: Lyyn Eakin and Associates, August.

Eakin, Lyyn, and Ted Richmond. 2004. "Community Service Organizations at Risk." *The Philanthropist Journal,* December 1. thephilanthropist.ca/2004/12/community.

Edwards, Michael. 2004. *Civil Society.* Cambridge, UK: Polity.

Elgenius, Gabriella. 2018. "Social Division and Resentment in the Aftermath of the Economic Slump." In *Austerity, Community Action, and the Future of Citizenship in Europe,* edited by Shana Cohen, Christina Fuhr and Jan-Jonathan Bock. 39–62. Bristol, UK: Policy Press.

Elson, Peter R. 2009. "Independence in a Cold Climate: A Profile of the Non-profit and Voluntary Sector in Canada." In *The First Principle of Voluntary Action,* edited by M. Smerdon, Baring Foundation. 13–34. baringfoundation.org.uk/wp-content/uploads/2014/09/FirstPrincipleofVA.pdf.

———. 2011. *High Ideals and Noble Intentions: Voluntary Sector-Government Relations in Canada.* Toronto, Buffalo, London: University of Toronto Press.

———. 2014. "Third Wave, Third Sector: Comparative Provincial Governance of Third Sector Relations." *Canadian Journal of Public Administration* 57, 4: 527–547.

——— (ed.). 2016. "Funding Policies and the Non-profit Sector in Western Canada." The Institute of Public Administration of Canada (IPAC) Series in Public Management and Governance. Toronto, Buffalo, London: University of Toronto Press.

Elson, Peter, and Peyton Carmichael. 2022. "A Short History of Voluntary Sector-Government Relations in Canada (Revisited)." *The Philanthropist Journal,* April 12. https://thephilanthropist.ca/2022/04/a-short-history-of-voluntary-sectorgovernment-relations-in-canada-revisited/.

Elson, P.R., P. Hall and P. Wamucii. 2016. *Canadian National Social Enterprise Sector Survey Report.* Mount Royal University, Institute for Community Prosperity and Simon Fraser University.

Emmett, Brian, and Geoffrey Emmett. 2015. *Charities in Canada as an Economic Sector: Discussion Paper.* Toronto: Imagine Canada.

Evans, Bryan. 2020. "The Politics of Public Administration: Constructing the

Neoliberal State." In *Canadian Political Economy,* edited by Heather Whiteside. 123–144. Toronto: University of Toronto Press.

Evans, Bryan, Ted Richmond, and John Shields. 2005. "Structuring Neoliberal Governance: The Non-profit Sector, Emerging New Modes of Control and the Marketisation of Service Delivery." *Policy and Society* 24, 1: 73–97.

Evans, Bryan, and John Shields. 2010. "The Third Sector and the Provision of Public Good: Partnerships, Contracting and the Neo-liberal State." In *The Handbook of Canadian Public Administration,* edited by Christopher Dunn. 305–318.Toronto: Oxford University Press.

___. 2014. "Non-Pofit Engagement with Provincial Policy Officials: The Case of Canadian Immigrant Settlement Services and NGO Policy Voice." *Policy and Society* 33, 2: 117–127.

___. 2018. "The Third Sector, the Neo-liberal State and Beyond: Reshaping Contracting and Policy Advocacy." In *The Handbook of Canadian Public Administration,* edited by Christopher Dunn. 489–500. Don Mills, ON: Oxford University Press.

Fairbairn, Brett. 2014. "Appendix: The Enterprise with Many Names: Establishing a Common Language." In *Co-operative Canada Empowering Communities and Sustainable Businesses,* edited by Fairbairn and Russell. Vancouver, BC: UBC Press.

Fairbairn, Brett, and Nora Russell (eds.). 2014. *Co-operative Canada Empowering Communities and Sustainable Businesses.* Vancouver, BC: UBC Press.

Farthing-Nichol, D., L. Lalande, and J. Cave. 2017. "Turning a Corner Laying the Groundwork for Charity Regulatory Reform in Canada." Mowat Research #150 Enabling Environment MowatNFP. niagaraknowledgeexchange.com/wp-content/uploads/sites/2/2017/06/150_EE_turning_a_corner.pdf.

Firempong, Jesse. 2018. "10,000 People Stand Strong to Protect Land and Water from Kinder Morgan." greenpeace.org/canada/en/story/630/10000-people-stand-strong-to-protect-land-and-water-from-kinder-morgan/.

Friesen, J. 2021. "University Donations of More than $10-Million Are on the Rise." *Globe and Mail,* January 25. A1 & A15.

Fumkin, Peter. 2009. *On Being Nonprofit: A Conceptual and Policy Primer.* Cambridge, MA: Harvard University Press.

Galley, A., E. McIsaac and J. Van Ymeren. 2014. "From Investment to Impact: The NFP Experience with Social Impact Bonds." Mowat Research #93. University of Toronto School of Public Policy & Governance.

Gamble, Andrew. 1988. *The Free Economy and the Strong State: The Politics of Thatcherism.* New York: Palgrave.

Gibbons, Roger 2016. "The Moral Imperative for Policy Advocacy, Part 3: Reflections on the Consultations." *The Philanthropist Journal,* August 8. thephilanthropist.ca/2016/08/the-moral-imperative-for-policy-advocacy-part-3-reflections-on-the-consultations/.

Gibson, K., S. O'Donnell, and V. Rideout. 2007. "The Project-Funding Regime: Complications for Community Organizations and their Staff." *Canadian Public Administration Journal* 50, 3. susanodo.ca/wp-content/uploads/2017/06/2007-CPAJ-Gibson.pdf.

Gingras, P., and M. Carrier. 2014. "Reclaiming Community: Co-operatives and Sectoral Governance in Quebec Forestry." In *Co-operative Canada Empowering Communities and Sustainable Businesses,* edited by B. Fairbairn and N. Russell. 139–157. Vancouver: UBC Press.

Gordon Foundation. n.d. "Who We Are." gordonfoundation.ca/.

Government of Canada. 2012. *Status of Co-operatives in Canada: Report of the Special Committee on Co-operatives.* Blake Richards, M.P., Chair 41st Parliament, First Session. canada.coop/wp-content/uploads/Special-COOP-committee-report-EN.pdf.

___. 2021a. "Report #3 of the Advisory Committee on the Charitable Sector - July 2021." canada.ca/en/revenue-agency/programs/about-canada-revenue-agency-cra/corporate-reports-information/advisory-committee-charitable-sector/report-advisory-committee-charitable-sector-july-2021.html.

___. 2021b. "About the Social Finance Fund." Employment and Social Development Canada. canada.ca/en/employment-social-development/programs/social-innovation-social-finance/social-finance-fund.html.

Government of Canada and Voluntary Sector. 1999. *Working Together: Report of the Joint Tables.* September 27. Ottawa: Queen's Printer.

Government of Ontario. 2013. *State of the Sector: Profile of Ontario Not-for-Profit and Charitable Organizations.* Ontario Ministry of Citizenship and Immigration with Pollara Strategic Insights. publications.gov.on.ca/state-of-the-sector-profile-of-ontario-not-for-profit-and-charitable-organizations-volume-i-overall-report.

Grand Council of the Crees. 2023. "MOU Establishing a Permanent Cree, Inuit and Naskapi Forum of Northers Québec." cngov.ca/mou-signing-permanent-forum/.

Greenfield, Patrick. 2021. "Indigenous Peoples Face Rise in Rights Abuses During Pandemic, Report Finds." *The Guardian,* February 18. https://www.theguardian.com/environment/2021/feb/18/indigenous-peoples-face-rise-in-rights-abuses-during-covid-pandemic-report-aoe.

Greenpeace. 2021. "Five of the Top Environmental Winds of 2021." greenpeace.org/canada/en/story/51632/five-top-environmental-wins-of-2021/.

Griffiths, R. 2020. "Kick-Starting Canada's Charities." *Globe and Mail,* December 21: B4.

Guo, Chao, and Wolfgang Bielefeld. 2014. "Social Entrepreneurship: An Evidence-Based Approach to Creating Social Value." San Francisco: John Wiley & Sons, Inc. wiley.com/en-ca/ Social+Entrepreneurship%3A+An+Evidence+Based+Approach+to+Creating+Social+Value-p-9781118844175.

Hacker, Jacob S. 2019. *The Great Risk Shift: The New Economic Insecurity and the Decline of the American Dream.* New York: Oxford University Press.

Hajer, Jesse. 2019. "Fast Facts: Social Impact Bonds A Costly Innovation." Canadian Centre for Policy Alternatives 'Fast Facts.'" *Winnipeg Free Press,* January 16.

Hall, M.H., C.W. Barr, M. Easwaramoorthy, L.M. Salamon, and S.W. Sokolowski. 2005. "The Canadian Non-profit and Voluntary Sector in Comparative Perspective." Johns Hopkins University, Government of Canada and Imagine Canada. sectorsource.ca/sites/default/files/resources/files/jhu_report_en.pdf.

Harper, Tim. 2023. "Meeting the Moment: The Philanthropist Journal Looks to the Future." *The Philanthropist Journal,* June 27. thephilanthropist.ca/2023/06/meeting-the-moment-the-philanthropist-journal-looks-to-the-future/.

Harvie, David, Geoff Lightfoot, Simon Lilley, and Kenneth Weir. 2021. "Social Investment Innovation and the 'Social Turn' of Neoliberal Finance." *Critical Perspectives on Accounting* 79.

Hayes, M. 2021. "Experts Hope Report Will Aid Ottawa in Tackling Gender-Based Violence." *Globe and Mail,* June 22: A4.
Hillel, Inez. 2022. "Charities and Nonprofits Forced to Adapt as Debt and Deficit Reduction becomes a Fiscal Priority." Imagine Canada, June 13. imaginecanada.ca/en/360/charities-nonprofits-forced-to-adapt-debt-and-deficit-reduction-becomes-fiscal-priority.
Houston, Sandy. 2020a. "Important Update from the Metcalf Foundation." Metcalf Foundation, May 19. metcalffoundation.com/metcalf-story/important-update-from-the-metcalf-foundation/.
———. 2020b. "Metcalf Foundation News." December 2020. metcalffoundation.com/newsletter/fall-2020-newsletter/.
Hughes, Ciaran, and Markus Ketola. 2021. *Neoliberalism and the Voluntary and Community Sector in Northern Ireland.* Bristol, UK: Policy Press.
Hunter, Justine. 2023. "For-Profit Care Facilities Underdeliver: BC Report." *Globe and Mail,* September 26.
IAAW (Institute for the Advancement of Aboriginal Women). n.d. "Our Stories." iaaw.ca/.
Imagine Canada. n.d. "Infographic: Canada's Charities & Nonprofits." imaginecanada.ca/sites/default/files/Infographic-sector-stat-2021.pdf.
———. 2018a. "30 Years of Giving in Canada: Who Gives, How, and Why? [Infographic]." April 9. imaginecanada.ca/en/360/30-years-giving-canada-who-gives-how-and-why-infographic.
———. 2018b. "The Impact of an Emerging Social Deficit on Charities and Nonprofits." July 4. imaginecanada.ca/en/360/impact-emerging-social-deficit-charities-and-nonprofits-infographic.
———. 2019. "Non-profit Sector Continues to Grow." March 5. imaginecanada.ca/en/360/non-profit-sector-continues-grow.
———. 2020a. *Are Charities Ready for Social Finance? Investment Readiness in Canada's Charitable Sector.* imaginecanada.ca/en/charities-social-finance-report-download.
———. 2020b. "HRCouncil.ca HR Toolkit Resources Coming Back!" August 26. imagine-canada.ca/en/360/hr-council-assets.
———. 2022. "Budget 2022: A Step Forward and New Opportunities for Collaboration with the Non-profit and Charitable Sector." April 7. imaginecanada.ca/en/news/budget-2022-a-step-forward-and-new-opportunities-for-collaboration.
———. 2023. "Shifting Power Dynamics: Equity, Diversity and Inclusion in the Non-profit Sector." Podcast. https://www.imaginecanada.ca/en/360/lets-imagine-podcast-episode-9-equity-diversity-inclusion-within-nonprofit-sector.
Imagine Canada and Ethnicity Matters. 2020. "Multicultural Canadians the Future of Generosity: Survey." Press release, September 01. imaginecanada.ca/en/360/multicultural-canadians-future-generosity-survey.
Imagine and PFC (Philanthropic Foundations Canada). 2014. "Assets and Giving Trends of Canada's Grantmaking Foundations." https://pfc.ca/publication/assets-giving-trends-of-canadas-grantmaking-foundations-september-2014/.
Indspire. n.d. "About Indspire." indspire.ca/.
Innovation, Science and Economic Development Canada. 2018 *Co-operatives in Canada,* 2015. https://publications.gc.ca/collections/collection_2019/isde-ised/Iu170-1-2015-eng.pdf.

International Monetary Fund. 2020. "COVID-19 Analytical Snapshot #33. Combating Xenophobia and Racism." March 8. https://www.iom.int/resources/covid-19-analytical-snapshot-33-combating-xenophobia-and-racism.

Intiar, Inda, and Njoki Mbũrũ. 2023. "Lessons from a Transformational Storytelling Fellowship." *The Philanthropist Journal*, August 21. thephilanthropist.ca/2023/08/lessons-from-a-transformational-storytelling-fellowship/.

IOM. 2021. *From Silos to Solutions: Toward Sustainable and Equitable Hybrid Service Delivery in the Immigrant & Refugee-Serving Sector in Canada.* iom.int/resources/silos-solutions-toward-sustainable-and-equitable-hybrid-service-delivery-immigrant-refugee-serving-sector-canada.

IRCC (Immigration, Refugees and Citizenship Canada). 2016. *Social Finance for the Settlement and Integration Sector.* Produced by Purpose Capital and Carleton Centre for Community Innovation. karimharji.com/wp-content/uploads/Social-Finance-for-Settlement-Sector.pdf.

Ireton, Julie. 2021. "Charities and Nonprofits in Trouble Seek Federal Support." *CBC News*, April 6.

Jäger, Anto. 2022. "From Bowling Alone to Posting Alone." *Jacobin* 47: 48–61.

Jensen, Emily. 2021. "Recent Data Releases from Statistics Canada Are Helpful but More Is Needed." Imagine Canada. imaginecanada.ca/en/360/recent-data-releases-statistics-canada-are-helpful-more-needed#:~:text=Recent%20data%20releases%20from%20Statistics%20Canada%20are%20helpful%20but%20more%20is%20needed,-Emily%20Jensen&text=Having%20accurate%20and%20up%2Dto,deficit%20for%20some%20time%20now.

___. 2023. "What Trends Will Impact Charities and Nonprofits in the First Quarter of 2023?" Imagine Canada, February 7. imaginecanada.ca/en/360/What-trends-will-impact-charities-and-nonprofits-in-the-first-quarter-of-2023.

Johnston, Patrick. 2013. "A Retrospective Look at the Voluntary Sector Initiative (VSI): What Lessons Did We Learn?" *The Philanthropist Journal*, February 20. thephilanthropist.ca/original-pdfs/Philanthropist-25-1-512.pdf.

Joy, Meghan, and John Shields. 2016. "Austerity in the Social Sector: Reconfiguring Citizenship through Social Impact Bonds." International Political Science Association Annual Conference. Poznan, Poland.

___. 2018. "Austerity in the Making: Reconfiguring Social Policy through Social Impact Bonds." *Policy and Politics* 46, 4: 681–695.

___. 2020. "The Political Economy of the Non-profit Sector." In *Canadian Political Economy*, edited by Heather Whiteside. 215–233. Toronto: University of Toronto Press.

Kelly, Katharine, and Tullio Caputo. 2011. *Community: A Contemporary Analysis of Policies, Programs and Practices.* Toronto: University of Toronto Press.

Ketilson, Lou Hammond. 2014. "To See Our Communities Come Alive Again with Pride: Re-inventing Co-operatives for First Nations' Needs." In *Co-operative Canada: Empowering Communities and Sustainable Businesses*, edited. by B. Fairbairn, and N. Russell. 209–233. Vancouver: UBC Press.

Kirkup, Kristy. 2020. "Off-Reserve Indigenous Services to Receive $75-million More in Federal Funds." *Globe and Mail*, March 21. https://www.theglobeandmail.com/politics/article-off-reserve-indigenous-services-to-receive-75-million-more-in-federal/.

Kirkup, Kristy, and Willow Fiddler. 2021. "Assembly of First Nations Election Nears." *Globe and Mail,* July 06: A7. https://go-gale-com.ezproxy.lib.torontomu.ca/ps/i.do?p=CPI&u=rpu_main&id=GALE%7CA667541018&v=2.1&it=r&sid=summon&aty=ip.

Kivel, P. 2017. "Social Services or Social Change?" In *The Revolution Will Not Be Funded: Beyond the Non-profit Industrial Complex,* edited by INCITE! 129–150. Durham, NC: Duke University Press,

Kochie, Dakota. 2022. "Turning the Page on an Ugly Chapter." *Globe and Mail* Opinion, January 10: A11.

Kovach, Margaret. 2021. *Indigenous Methodologies: Characteristics, Conversations, and Context.* Halifax: Fernwood Publishing.

Laforest, Rachel. 2011a. "L'étude du tiers secteur au Québec: Comment saisir la spécificité québécoise?" *Politique et Sociétés* 30, 1: 43–45.

___. 2011b. *Voluntary Sector Organizations and the State Building New Relations.* Vancouver: UBC Press.

Lasby, David. 2020. "Imagine Canada's Sector Monitor: Charities & the COVID-19 Pandemic." May. https://www.imaginecanada.ca/sites/default/files/COVID-19%20Sector%20Monitor%20Report%20ENGLISH_0.pdf.

___. 2021. "Ongoing Effects of the COVID-19 Pandemic." Imagine Canada's Sector Monitor. imaginecanada.ca/sites/default/files/Sector-Monitor-Ongoing-Effects-COVID-19-Pandemic-EN.pdf.

Lasch, Christopher. 1995. *The Revolt of the Elites and the Betrayal of Democracy.* New York: W.W. Norton & Company.

Lauer, Sean, Karen Lok Yi Wong and Miu Chung Yan. 2022. *Making Friends at Community Organizations: How Do Place-Based Community Organizations Promote Friendship Formation?* Vancouver: University of British Columbia. ifsnetwork.org/wp-content/uploads/2023/05/Making-frineds-at-commuity-orgnaizations.pdf.

Lawson Foundation. 2016. "Journey to Reconciliation Webinar Series Launched." Press Release. https://lawson.ca/journey-to-reconciliation-webinar-series-launched/.

Leary, John Patrick. 2018. *Keywords: The New Language of Capitalism.* Halifax: Fernwood Publishing.

Liao, Carol. 2017. "The Changing Face of the Non-profit Sector: Social Enterprise Legislation in British Columbia." In *Shifting Terrain: Non-profit Policy Advocacy in Canada,* edited by N.J. Mulé and G.C. DeSantis. McGill Queens University Press.

Lorentzen, Christian. 2022. "The Hopeful Dystopian: On the Enduring Appeal of Christopher Lasch — On Both Left and Right." *Jacobin* 47 (Fall): 23–31.

Lorinc, John. 2019. "Canada's Charitable Sector: What to Expect in 2019." *The Philanthropist Journal,* January 07. thephilanthropist.ca/2019/01/canadas-charitable-sector-what-to-expect-in-2019/.

Lowe, S., T. Richmond, and J. Shields. 2017. "Settling on Austerity: ISAs, Immigrant Communities and Neoliberal Restructuring." *Alternate Routes: A Journal of Critical Social Research* 28: 14–46. alternateroutes.ca/index.php/ar/article/view/22417.

Lui, Stephanie. 2021. "'Enormous amount of change': New data reveals impact of COVID-19 on Canadians." *CTV News,* March 11 https://www.ctvnews.ca/health/coronavirus/

enormous-amount-of-change-new-data-reveals-impact-of-covid-19-on-canadians-1.5343991.

MacDonald, Bruce. 2022. "Towards a More Just and Equitable Society: Where We Are Now. An Update from Imagine Canada on Anti-Racism and Anti-Oppression." Imagine Canada, October 03. imaginecanada.ca/en/Towards-a-more-just-and-equitable-society-where-we-are-now.

Mayne, J. 2001. "Addressing Attribution Through Contribution Analysis: Using Performance Measures Sensibly." *Canadian Journal of Program Evaluation* 16, 1: 1–24.

McBride, Stephen, and John Shields. 1997. *Dismantling a Nation: The Transition to Corporate Rule in Canada,* 2nd edition. Halifax: Fernwood Publishing.

McCabe, Angus, and Jenny Phillimore. 2018. *Community Groups in Context: Local Activities and Actions.* Bristol: Policy Press.

McGoey, Linsey. 2015. *No Such Thing as a Free Gift: The Gates Foundation and the Price of Philanthropy.* London: Verso.

McIsaac, E., S. Park, and L. Toupin. 2013. *Shaping the Future: Leadership in Ontario's Non-profit Labour Force.* The Mowat Center, University of Toronto. theonn.ca/wp-content/uploads/2013/12/ONN-Mowat.Shaping-the-Future.-Leadership.Exec-Summary.pdf.

McKnight, Brent, and Julie Gouweloos. 2021. "How COVID-19 Could Transform Non-profit Organizations." *The Conversation,* January 31.

McNeill, Andrew. 2013. "Human Resources Minister Diane Finley Is Right to Pursue Social Impact Bonds: Editorial." *Toronto Star,* May 8.

Mendell, Marguerite, and Nancy Neamtan. 2010. "The Social Economy in Quebec: Towards a New Political Economy." In *Researching the Social Economy,* edited by L. Mook, J Quarter and S. Ryan. 63–83. University of Toronto Press.

Métis National Council. n.d. "Governance." metisnation.ca/about/governance.

Milligan, C., and N. Fyfe. 2005. "Preserving Space for Volunteers: Exploring the Links Between Voluntary Welfare Organizations, Volunteering, and Citizenship." *Urban Studies* 42, 3: 417–433.

Mulé, Nick J., and Gloria C. Desantis (eds.). 2017. *The Shifting Terrain: Non-profit Policy Advocacy in Canada.* Montreal and Kingston – London – Chicago: McGill-Queens University Press.

Muttart Foundation. 2013. *Talking About Charities.* muttart.org/resource/talking-about-charities-2013-news-release/.

Nakua, Abdul. 2023. "Combatting Polarization by Transforming Anger Into Action." *The Philanthropist Journal,* January 27. thephilanthropist.ca/2023/01/combatting-polarization-by-transforming-anger-into-action/.

Nanos, Nik. 2020. "Data Dive with Nik Nanos: How the Pandemic Could Devastate the Charitable Sector." *Globe and Mail,* December 11.

NWAC (Native Women's Association of Canada). n.d. "About." nwac.ca/about-us.

OECD (Organisation for Economic Co-operation and Development). 2003. *The Non-profit Sector in a Changing Economy.* read. oecd-ilibrary.org/urban-rural-and-regional-development/the-non-profit-sector-in-a-changing-economy_9789264199545-en#page1.

Omidvar, Ratna. 2020. "Government Should Change Outmoded Fundraising Rules for Charities." *Policy Options,* September

8. policyoptions.irpp.org/magazines/september-2020/government-should-change-outmoded-fundraising-rules-for-charities/.

Omidvar, Ratna, and Ted Richmond. 2003. *Immigrant Settlement and Social Inclusion in Canada*. Toronto: Laidlaw Foundation. laidlawfdn.org/assets/wpsosi_2003_jan_immigrant-settlement.pdf.

ONN (Ontario Nonprofit Network). n.d.a. "Decent Work." theonn.ca/topics/policy-priorities/people/decent-work/.

———. n.d.b. Priority: Funding Reform. theonn.ca/topics/policy-priorities/financing/funding-reform/.

———. 2023. *State of the Sector: At a Tipping Point*. https://theonn.ca/publication/2023-state-of-the-sector-survey-policy-report/.

ONN (Ontario Nonprofit Network) and AFO (Assemblée de la francophonie de l'Ontario). 2020. *Risk, Resilience, and Rebuilding Communities: The State of Ontario Nonprofits Three Months into the Pandemic*. August. theonn.ca/wp-content/uploads/2020/08/Final_-English_-Three-months-into- covid-1.pdf.

———. 2021. *5 Ways Settler-Led Nonprofits Can Support Indigenous Communities*. theonn.ca/2021/06/5-ways-settler-led-nonprofits-can-support-indigenous-communities/.

———. 2022. *2022 State of the Sector During Uncertain Times*. theonn.ca/publication/2022-state-of-the-sector-policy-report/.

Osborne, David, and Ted Gaebler. 1992. *Reinventing Government: How the Entrepreneurial Spirit Is Transforming the Public Sector*. New York: Penguin Press.

Ott, J. Steven. 2001. "Introduction to the Nonprofit Sector." In *The Nature of the Nonprofit Sector*, edited by J. Steven Ott. 1–8. Boulder, CO: Westview Press.

Parachin, A. 2021. "Liberals Bid to Reform Charity Sector Falls Short." *Globe and Mail*, June 25: B7.

Pawelski, Ele. 2015. "Challenges to Implementing Social Financing Policy in Canada." *The Philanthropist Journal*, May 5. thephilanthropist.ca/2015/05/challenges-to-implementing-social-finance-policy-in-canada/.

Peck, J., and N. Theodore. 2019. "Still Neoliberalism?" *South Atlantic Quarterly* 118, 2: 245–265. doi.org/10.1215/00382876-7381122.

Pestoff, Victor, Taco Brandsen, and Bram Verschuere. 2011. *New Public Governance, the Third Sector, and Co-Production*. New York: Routledge.

PFC (Philanthropic Foundations Canada). 2017. *A Portrait of Canadian Foundation Philanthropy*. pfc.ca/wp-content/uploads/2022/01/portrait-cdn-philanthropy-sept2017-en.pdf.

———. 2021. "About PFC" and "Canadian Foundation Facts." https://pfc.ca.

Phillips, Susan D. 2016. "Funding Regimes: From the Outside Looking In." In *Funding Policies and the Nonprofit Sector in Western Canada*, edited by Peter R. Elson. The Institute of Public Administration of Canada (IPAC) Series in Public Management and Governance. Toronto, Buffalo, London: University of Toronto Press.

Piller, Thomas. 2019. "Sweet Dreams Home for At-Risk Mothers Exceeding Expectations in Saskatoon." *Global News*, June 27. globalnews.ca/news/5440180/sweet-dreams-saskatoon/.

Preston, Valerie, John Shields and Jayesh D'Souza. 2024. "Transforming Settlement and Integration Services During a Pandemic." *International Migration*, March 11: https://doi.org/10.1111/imig.13245.

Preston, Valerie, John Shields, and Marshia Akbar. 2022. "Migration and Resilience

in Urban Canada: Why Social Resilience, Why Now?" *Journal of International Migration and Integration* 23, 3: 1421–1441.
Procyk, Stephanie, Wayne Lewchuk, and John Shields (eds.). 2017. *Precarious Employment: Causes, Consequences and Remedies.* Halifax: Fernwood Publishing.
Putnam, Robert. 2000. *Bowling Alone: The Collapse and Revival of American Community.* New York: Simon & Schuster.
Raven. n.d. "Raven: Respecting Aboriginal Values and Environmental Needs." raventrust.com/.
Reimer, Will. 2021. "Food Bank Use in Canada Climbed 20% During Pandemic, Report Shows." *Global News,* October 31.
Richmond, T., and A. Saloojee. 2005. *Social Inclusion Canadian Perspectives.* Fernwood Publishing.
Richmond, T., and J. Shields. 2004. "Third Sector Restructuring and the New Contracting Regime: The Case of Immigrant Serving Organizations in Ontario." CERIS Policy Matters, 3.
___. 2005. "NGO–Government Relations and Immigrant Services: Contradictions and Challenges." *Journal of International Migration and Integration* 6, 3–4 (Fall).
Rodney, Yvonne. 2023a. "The Future of Non-profit Work and Workers Post-Pandemic." *The Philanthropist Journal,* January 9. thephilanthropist.ca/2023/01/the-future-of-non-profit-work-and-workers-post-pandemic/.
___. 2023b. "Volunteerism: In Crisis or at a Crossroads?" *The Philanthropist Journal,* March 14. thephilanthropist.ca/2023/03/volunteerism-in-crisis-or-at-a-crossroads/.
Rodriguez, Melanie. 2020. "Health Nonprofits Face the Greatest Financial Challenge in History." ONN Blog, July 22.
Roelofs, Joan. 1995. "The Third Sector as a Protective Layer for Capitalism." *Monthly Review* 47, 4: 16–25.
Salamon, Lester. 1995. *Partners in Public Service Government-Non-profit Relations in the Modern Welfare State.* Baltimore, MD: Johns Hopkins University Press.
___. 1999. *America's Non-profit Sector: A Primer.* Ann Arbor, Michigan: Foundation Centre, University of Michigan.
Salamon, Lester, and Helmut K. Anheir. 1997. *Defining the Nonprofit Sector: A Cross-National Analysis.* Manchester: Manchester University Press.
Saunders, Ron. 2004. *Passion and Commitment Under Stress: Human Resource Issues in Canada's Non-profit Sector – A Synthesis Report.* CPRN Research Series on Human Resources in the Non-profit Sector.
Schaper, Bill. 2019. *Towards a 'Home in Government' for the Charitable and Non-profit Sector.* Imagine Canada. drive.google.com/file/d/15M_4PvSh7HzC8Srk4N5ojsrTRDjk4fKz/view.
Scott, Katherine. 2003. *Funding Matters: The Impact of Canada's New Funding Regime on Non-profit and Voluntary Organizations (Summary Report).* Canadian Council on Social Development. researchgate.net/publication/254343618_Funding_Matters_The_Impact_of_Canada's_New_Funding_Regime_on_Nonprofit_and_Voluntary_Organizations.
Settlement Sector & Technology Task Group. 2020. *Preliminary Report.* December 21. km4s.ca/wp-content/uploads/Settlement-Sector-Technology-Task-Group-Preliminary-Report-December-21-2020.pdf.

Shields, John. 2005. "The New NGO Funding Regime: Building Accountability, Human Resources and Civil Society in Canada?" The Network of East Vancouver Community Organizations Third Annual Conference, Vancouver, BC, June 14.

———. 2013. "Non-profit Engagement with Provincial Policy Officials: The Case of Canadian Immigrant Settlement Services." 1st International Conference on Public Policy, Grenoble.

———. 2014. "Constructing and 'Liberating' Temporariness in the Canadian Non-profit Sector: Neoliberalism and Non-profit Service Providers." In *Liberating Temporariness? Migration, Work and Citizenship in an Age of Insecurity*, edited by Robert Latham, Valerie Preston, and Leah Vosko. 255–281. Montreal: McGill-Queen's University Press.

———. 2019. "Evidence." *Catalyst for Change: A Roadmap to a Stronger Charitable Sector.* Report of the Special Senate Committee on the Charitable Sector. https://sencanada.ca/en/Content/SEN/Committee/421/cssb/54630-e.

Shields, John, and Zainab Abu Alrob. 2021. "The Political Economy of a Modern Pandemic: Assessing Impacts of COVID-19 on Migrants and Immigrants in Canada." Alternate Routes: A Journal of Critical Social Research 32, 1: 137–161.

Shields, John, Ian Cunningham, and Donna Baines. 2017. "Precarious Undertakings: Serving Vulnerable Communities through Non-profit Work." In *Precarious Employment: Causes, Consequences and Remedies*, edited by Stephanie Procyk, Wayne Lewchuk, and John Shields. 31–43. Halifax, NS: Fernwood Publishing.

Shields, John, and B. Mitchell Evans. 1998. *Shrinking the State Globalization and Public Administration.* Halifax, NS: Fernwood Publishing.

Shields, John, Meghan Joy and Siu Mee Cheng. 2024. "The Limits of Community Nonprofit Sector Resilience: Evidence from Canadian Nonprofit Sector Surveys During the Pandemic." *Canadian Journal of Nonprofit and Social Economy Research/Revue canadienne de recherche sur les OBSL et l'économie sociale*, 15, 1.

Shields, John, Valerie Preston, and Jayesh D'Souza. 2022. "The Future of the Ontario Settlement Sector: Learning from a Global Pandemic." BMRC-IRMU Webinair (Building Migrant Resilience in Cities), May 5. YouTube Video. youtube.com/watch?v=BQugGClSgyc.

———. 2023. "Transforming Settlement and Integration Services During a Pandemic." Panel: Honouring Joe Garcea II: Membership, Multiculturalism, and Migration, Prairie Political Science Association 14th Annual Conference, Banff Centre, Banff, AB, September 22–24.

Singh Kelsall, Tyson, Jake Seaby Palmour, Rory Marck, A.J. Withers, Nicole Luongo, Kahlied Salem, Cassie Sutherland, Jasmine Veark, Lyana Patrick, Aaron Bailey, et al. 2023. "Situating the Nonprofit Industrial Complex." *Social Sciences* 12, 10: 549. https://doi.org/10.3390/socsci12100549.

Special Senate Committee on the Charitable Sector. 2019. *Catalyst for Change: A Roadmap to a Stronger Charitable Sector.* Report of the Special Senate Committee on the Charitable Sector. Ottawa: Senate, June. https://sencanada.ca/content/sen/committee/421/CSSB/Reports/CSSB_Report_Final_e.pdf.

SPT (Social Planning Toronto). 2020. *Q&A on COVID-19 Income & Housing Supports—Now in 15 Languages!* June 16. www.socialplanningtoronto.org/15_languages_covid_supports.

Stadelmann-Elder, Markus. 2021. *New and Affordable Option for Nonprofits to Build*

Retirement Security for Their Employees: The Common Good Plan. March 24. maytree.com/publications/retirement-security-common-good-plan/.

Statistics Canada. 2004. *Cornerstones of Community: Highlights of the National Survey of Non-profit and Voluntary Organizations.* www150.statcan.gc.ca/n1/pub/61-533-x/2004001/4069554-eng.htm.

——. 2008. *Satellite Account of Non-profit Institutions and Volunteering 1997 to 2005.* www150.statcan.gc.ca/n1/en/pub/13-015-x/13-015-x2008000-eng.pdf?st=-mGz1Piw.

——. 2012. *Charitable Giving by Canadians.* www150.statcan.gc.ca/n1/pub/11-008-x/2012001/article/11637-eng.htm.

——. 2019a. *Co-operatives in Canada 2018.* www150.statcan.gc.ca/n1/pub/11-627-m/11-627-m2019087-eng.htm.

——. 2019b. *Non-profit Institutions and Volunteering: Economic Contribution 2007 to 2017.* www150.statcan.gc.ca/n1/daily-quotidien/190305/dq190305a-eng.htm.

Stueck, W. 2021. "Bond to Tackle Diabetes in First Nations Communities." *Globe and Mail,* March 03: B1 & B6.

Taylor, Marilyn. 2002. "Government, the Third Sector and the Contract Culture: The UK Experience So Far." In Dilemmas of the Welfare Mix: The New Structure of Welfare in an Era of Privatization, edited by Ugo Ascoli and Constanzo Ranci. 77–88. New York: Kluwer Academic/Plenum Publishers.

Taylor, Paul. 2021. "To Truly Make an Impact, Nonprofits and Charities Must Push for Political Change." *Globe and Mail,* April 23. Link expired.

Thomas, Derrick. 2012. "Giving and Volunteering among Canada's Immigrants." Canadian Social Trends. Statistics Canada. www150.statcan.gc.ca/n1/en/catalogue/11-008-X201200111669.

Thompson, Matthew, and Joy Emmanuel. 2012. *Assembling Understandings: Findings from the Canadian Social Economy Research Partnerships 2005–2011.* University of Victoria. dspace.library.uvic.ca/bitstream/handle/1828/3879/au_book_final_April122012.pdf?sequence=15&isAllowed=y.

Tiwari, S. 2021. "Raven Indigenous Capital Helps Entrepreneurs Take Flight." *Corporate Knights* (Spring). corporateknights.com/leadership/raven-indigenous-capital-helps-entrepreneurs-take-flight/.

Tombe, Trevor, and Daniel Béland. 2022. "The Federal Budget Missed an Opportunity to Renew Canada's Federation." *Globe and Mail* Opinion, April 8. https://www.theglobeandmail.com/opinion/article-the-federal-budget-missed-an-opportunity-to-renew-canadas-federation/.

Toronto Non-profit Network. 2020. "Tell the Pm We Need Relief. Now." Open letter to Prime Minister Justin Trudeau. www.torontononprofits.org/call_to_action_sector_relief.

Truth and Reconciliation Commission of Canada. 2015. "Calls to Action." www2.gov.bc.ca/assets/gov/british-columbians-our-governments/indigenous-people/aboriginal-peoples-documents/calls_to_action_english2.pdf.

Vézina, M., and S. Crompton. 2012. *Volunteering in Canada.* Canadian Social Trends. Statistics Canada.

Volunteer Canada, Volunteer Management Professionals of Canada and spinktank. 2020. "The Volunteering Lens of COVID-19: Fall 2020 Survey – Impacts of COVID-19 on Volunteer Engagement." December. volunteer.ca/vdemo/

ResearchAndResources_DOCS/Vol%20Lens%202020%20Survey%20Results/VC_FallSurveyReport_2020_ENG_FINAL.pdf.
Waldie, Paul. 2020. "COVID-19 Pandemic Has Exposed Deep Flaws in Canadian Philanthropy, Fragility of Nonprofits." *Globe and Mail,* December 12.
___. 2021. "Couple Guided by Reconciliation with Donation to Health Centre." *Globe and Mail,* July 03: B2.
Walsh, Kieron. 1995. *Public Services and Market Mechanisms: Competition, Contracting and the New Public Management.* New York: St. Martin's Press.
Ware, Robert. 1999. "Public Moral Values, the Fabrication of Communities and Disempowerment." In *Citizens or Consumers? Social Policy in Market Society,* edited by W. Anthony and D. Broad. 299–312. Halifax, NS: Fernwood Publishing.
White, Patrick. 2022. "First Nation in Saskatchewan Finds 54 Possible Unmarked Graves Near Former Residential Schools." *Globe and Mail,* February 14.
Whiteside, Heather. 2020. "Introduction: Changes, Crises, and Conflicts in Canadian Political Economy." In *Canadian Political Economy,* edited by Heather Whiteside. 3–22. Toronto: University of Toronto Press.
Wiig, Siri, and Babette Fahlbruch. 2019. "Exploring Resilience — An Introduction." In *Exploring Resilience: A Scientific Journey from Practice to Theory,* edited by S. Wiig and B. Fahlbruch. 1–5. Cham, Switzerland: Springer Open.
Wolch, J. 1990. *Shadow State: Government and Voluntary Sector in Transition.* New York: Foundation Center.
YMCA. 2021. "YMCAs in Canada Statement of Reconciliation." ymcaywca.ca/about-us/statement-of-reconciliation.
York, Geoffrey. 2021. "Canadian Charity Gives a Billion-Dollar Boost to Africa's Worsening COVID-19 Vaccine Crisis." *Globe and Mail,* June 09: A1.

Index

Access Alliance, 1–2
accountability, 38
    administrative versus public, 64, 66–7, 106
    contract funding and, 64, 66–8, 95–6
    multi-directional versus funder-focused, 14, 64, 66, 80, 110–11
    neoliberal restructuring impacts, 10, 13–14, 110–11
    voluntary sector, 71–2, 74
advocacy,
    big versus small, 69
    chill, 70–1, 77, 80–3
    concepts and forms of, 69, 71, 81
    coordination, 81–2, 114, 116
    amid COVID-19: 93–4, 107–8
    Indigenous rights, 85–90, 109
    member-funded, 83–4
    neoliberal restructuring impacts, 10, 66, 69–70, 114–17
    non-profit mission-based, 10, 24, 41–3, 69, 83, 89, 110
    organizational focus on, 30, 32, 70, 81–2, 112
    policy, 42, 70–2, 82
    repression of, 70–1, 73–6, 89–90, 116–17
    social justice/human rights, 16, 18, 20, 27, 44, 106–7, 114
    variable support for, 39–40, 45, 84–6
Affiliation of Multicultural Societies and Service Agencies (AMSSA, BC), 83, 100
African Nova Scotians, 105
agencies, 87
    COVID-19 impacts, 91–6, 98–101, 107, 117
    funding of, 5, 63, 66–7, 93–6, 107–8
    immigrant service (ISAs), 83, 93–6, 99
    new public management and, 12, 14, 96
    non-profit, 23, 27, 43, 81, 93–8, 105
    organizational structure, 5, 22–3, 98
alternative service delivery (ASD), 12–14, 17
Amnesty International, 84, 103–4
    No More Stolen Sisters campaign, 89, 90n5
Anheir, Helmut, 22–3
anti-Black racism, 9, 43, 91, 102–3, 106
anti-racism, 43, 102–3, 104–7
    see also anti-Black racism; racism
Assembly of First Nations, 86–7, 90n5
Atkinson Foundation, 61, 85
austerity, 26n1, 51
    destabilizing amid COVID-19: 96, 102
    non-profit functioning under, 20, 62, 113, 119

Barr, Cathy, 115–16
Béland, Daniel, 86
Black Lives Matter, 4, 105, 112–13
Black people, 50, 104–5
    presence in non-profit sector, 57, 76, 82, 102
    racism facing, *see* anti-Black racism
Blackstock, Cindy, 87
Brock, Kathy, 71, 73

CanadaHelps, 48–9, 82
Canada Revenue Agency (CRA),
    advocacy regulation and, 70, 73, 77–80
    nonprofits reporting to, 26, 85

capacity,
    challenges in building, 27, 31, 68, 98–102
    decision-making, 23, 53, 101, 108
    demand versus, 98, 108, 119–20
    funding and, 50, 63, 98–101, 113, 118
    nonprofits' limitations on, 6, 14–16, 77, 94, 109
    resilience and, 7, 68, 98, 114
    to do more with less, 7, 14, 16, 62, 68
Capacity Joint Table, 72–4
capital, 72
    human, 11, 56, 59
    investment, 15, 34, 38, 54
    private, 51–2, 54
    social, 20, 36
    social finance, 54–6
capitalism,
    neoliberal, 10, 56, 113
    non-profit role in, 20, 56, 111
centralized decentralization, 13–14, 64
charitable sector, 114
    data on, 19, 26, 28–32, 39–40, 46–7
    funding, 47–50, 91, 97, 107, 118
    increasing reliance on, 6, 24, 82, 107, 119
    resource challenges in, 60–2, 68, 70, 94–5, 113, 118–19
    social finance and, 51, 45–5
    Voluntary Sector Initiative (VSI) process, 73–4
    see also Special Senate Committee on the Charitable Sector report
charities,
    Canadian support for, 39, 48, 50–1
    COVID-19 impacts on, 91–5, 97–8, 107
    increasing number of, 25, 39–41, 82
    Indigenous-focused, 49, 87–8
    nonprofits versus, 5, 18–19, 43, 84
    registered versus non-incorporated, 19, 26–30, 32, 42, 73, 78–9
    regulation of, 77–81, 85, 89–90
    see also donations
childcare,
    funding, 5, 82
    service provision, 4–5, 38, 119

child and family services nonprofits, 32, 47, 87
citizenship, 17, 19
    nonprofits' support for, 16, 25, 38, 112
civil society,
    concept of, 14
    neoliberalism versus, 10, 14–15, 71, 113
    nonprofits' role in, 12n1, 15–17, 20, 25, 41, 101, 110
Clutterbuck, Peter, 60–1
Coates, Ken, 89
Colbourne, Tyler, 65–6
communities,
    approaches centring specific, 13, 43, 54, 87–90, 97, 105
    charitable support for, 49–50, 60, 64, 82, 87–8, 119
    government shifting risks to, 10–11, 110–11, 119
    neoliberalism versus, 8, 14–15, 39, 45, 111–13
    nonprofits' accountability to, 14–16, 24–5, 34, 64, 66, 80, 109
    nonprofits' presence in, 20, 25, 30–1, 68, 94, 100
    nonprofits meeting needs of, 5, 17, 29, 62, 71, 101–2
    reaching marginalized, 28–30, 50–5, 76–7, 116, 120
    serving vulnerable, 19, 41, 62, 68–9, 92, 107–12
    values of market versus, 14–15, 34, 36–8
    voice of, *see* voice
    see also civil society
community foundations, 39–41, 61
Community Foundations of Canada (CFC), 40–1, 59, 88
Conservative governments, 26n1, 54, 70, 83
contract funding, 51, 95–6
    advocacy efforts versus, 70, 80
    control through, 13, 64–7, 80–1, 110–11
    problems of, 46, 62–6, 115–17
    regime, 63–6, 80, 109
    shortfalls in, 14, 62–4, 68, 119

contracts,
  accountability conditions of, 66–7
  competitive tendering, 2, 13, 45, 51
  worker precarity on, 37, 39, 62–6, 68, 109
cooperatives, 5, 42, 65
  community roles of, 35–6, 51
  data on non-financial, 33–5
  objectives and principles of, 33–5
  in Quebec, 38–9
  representative organizations of, 35–6
  support for, 55–6
COVID-19 pandemic,
  calls for government stabilization in, 93–6, 113
  challenges after, 96, 113, 117–19
  collaboration in, 107–8, 113
  donations and philanthropy amid, 49, 92–3, 97, 105, 107
  funding impacts in, 55, 91–3, 97–8
  lessons from, 16, 96, 99–102, 107–9, 113, 117
  nonprofits amid, 16, 31, 61, 95–101
  polarization from, 45, 101–2
  shift to virtual service provision, 16, 49, 95, 98–100, 107
credit unions, 5, 55–6
  data on, 33–5, 38–9
critical political economy (CPE), 2, 19
culture and recreation nonprofits, 32, 47, 58

demand for services, 51, 116–17
  COVID-19 and, 91–4, 98
  weakening nonprofits' capacity, 2, 45, 108, 113, 119
democracy, 86
  cooperative functioning and, 34–5
  crisis of, 10, 53
  facilitating engagement with, 20, 24, 110
  neoliberalism versus, 66, 70–1
  nonprofits' role in, 10, 17, 38, 69, 120
Desantis, Gloria, 70–1, 76, 80
DeVerteuil, Geoffrey, 112
de Tocqueville, Alexis, 17

diversity,
  challenges with sector, 71, 75, 114
  increasing social, 42, 60–1, 65, 86, 105–9
  non-profit sector, 22–5, 27, 29, 66, 81–4, 110
donations,
  COVID-19 impacts on, 91, 95, 107, 118
  decline in smaller charity, 49–51, 68
  as funding source, 14, 46–51, 54, 92–3
  importance of, 48, 50–1, 56, 64, 83
  international, 48–9
  organizational screening of, 83–4
donees, 39–40, 87
  rules for non-qualified, 78–80
donors, financial, 66, 115
  control of, 39–41, 99
  data on individual, 47–50
  tax credits for, 28, 48–50
Douglas, Debbie, 99–100
D'Souza, Jayesh, 93, 95, 98

education nonprofits, 27, 31–2, 40–1, 47–8, 85–7
Edwards, Michael, 15
Elson, Peter, 28, 71, 73, 77–8, 80–1, 83
employees, non-profit,
  benefits plans for, 59–61
  compensation for, 57, 60–1
  contract, *see* contracts
  full-time, 37, 59–60, 63–4
  part-time, 37, 57–8, 62–3
  unpaid, 34
  working conditions, 58–9, 62, 92
employment,
  funding based on client, 8, 36
  lack of, 2, 11
  non-profit sector, 34, 37, 56–62, 65
  permanently temporary, 8, 64, 68
  precarious, *see* labour
  reduced funding impacts on, 59, 61–4
  training, 8, 34, 37, 52, 59–60, 81
entrepreneurialism, valuing of, 11, 17–18
environmental organizing, 4, 10, 27, 30, 36, 41, 93

Indigenous, 88–9
  potential muzzling of, 70, 80, 84–5, 90
equity, diversity and inclusion (EDI), 106–7
Europe, 37, 51, 104
evaluation,
  accountability versus, 66–8, 79
  lack of resources for, 67–8, 107

Fairbairn, Brett, 35–8
financial crisis, global (2008–2009): 30, 51, 113
First Nations Child and Family Caring Society, 87–8
Floyd, George, 102–3
food banks, 4, 6, 27, 109–12
funders,
  accountability to, 10, 14, 66, 69, 110–11
  control of, 13, 18, 64–6
  COVID-19 responses, 93–4, 96–9, 108
  expectations of, 18, 64, 66–7, 114, 118
  government, 26, 39, 64–5, 80–2, 110–11, 118
  philanthropic, 39, 41, 49–50, 61
funding,
  contract, *see* contract funding
  COVID-19 responses: 91, 93–7, 101–2, 108–9
  cuts to, 64, 70–1, 80, 90–1, 99, 107–8
  efforts to secure, 68, 72–3, 83–4, 101
  gaps, filling, 14, 16, 49–50, 64
  impacts, 18, 27–8, 67–8, 116–17
  insecure, 7, 30–2, 72, 98, 107
  monitoring of, 64–6, 78–9, 96, 113–16
  neoliberalism and, 8, 16, 39, 63–4, 101–2, 109–13
  precarious, *see* precarity
  project versus program, 8, 63–5, 111
  service-focused, 5, 12, 43, 99–100, 107
  shortfalls in, 14, 32, 59, 64
  social finance, 52, 54–6
  state, 5, 18, 23, 28, 54, 69–71, 82
  variable sources of, 37, 46–8, 68, 111
  see also donations; donors; Voluntary Sector Initiative (VSI)

fundraising, 4, 27, 65
  ongoing concerns of, 30, 50–1
  organizational facilitation of, 48, 87
  varying capacity for, 47, 49–50, 91, 93

Galley, Andrew, 52
Gamble, Andrew, 13
Gladu, JP, 89
Gordon Foundation, 88–9
government,
  agencies, 5, 83, 93–6, 99
  funding, 5, 18, 23, 28, 54, 69–71, 82
  non-profit institutions, 25, 32–3, 47, 57
  non-profit partnerships, 6, 12–13, 23–4, 52, 69–70, 83
  see also state, the
grants,
  applying for, 27, 31, 64, 83–4
  conditions attached to, 66, 68, 78, 106
  COVID-19 responses: 94, 96–7
  data on, 40, 47, 96
  funding from, 2, 37, 85, 88, 94, 97
  non-government versus government, 19, 39, 46–7
Greenpeace, 84, 89

Hajer, Jesse, 52–3
Harper, Stephen, 26n1, 70, 75, 80
health care, 3, 47, 61, 119
  COVID-19 and: 92–7, 107
  funding/compensation for, 18, 24, 53–4, 61, 66–8, 95–7
  limitations on access to, 6–7, 10, 92, 98
  neoliberal threat to, 14–15
  nonprofits, 4, 8, 27, 31–4, 40–1, 82–5, 98
homelessness, 4, 6, 20, 41
housing, 10, 83
  funding support for, 40, 52, 101
  nonprofits' focus on, 27, 31, 41–2, 114
  precarity, 7, 101, 116
Houston, Sandy, 97
human resources,
  funding for, 45–6, 63, 107

non-profit-sector issues, 58–61, 65, 106, 109, 117–19
undervaluing of, 56–7
human rights, nonprofits' advocacy for, 16, 44, 70, 84–5

Imagine Canada, 94, 119
  donation/funding data, 40–1, 48, 50, 92, 95–8
  initiatives of, 59, 80–2, 106, 113–15
immigrants, 15, 50
  charity involvement, 50
  discrimination/racism facing, 102, 106
  service provision for, 28, 31, 82–3, 93–6
  status of, 19, 101
  transitional needs of, 2, 41–3, 61
Immigration, Refugees and Citizenship Canada (IRCC), 55, 77, 95–6, 98–100
Indigenous peoples,
  advocacy for, 86–90, 102–5, 109, 114, 116
  charities for, 41, 49, 79, 87
  child welfare system involvement, 52, 87–8
  COVID-19 and, 96, 102
  environmentalism and, 88–9
  mobilization, 85–6, 89, 102, 112–13
  nonprofits focused on, 86–9, 102, 104–5, 114, 116
  racism facing, 43, 102, 104–5, 109
  reconciliation efforts, 41, 88–9, 102–5, 107
  representation in nonprofits, 57, 76, 87–9, 114
  rights, struggles for, 9, 81, 85–9, 91, 102–6
  social impact bond programming, 52, 54
  social service provision, 42–3, 85–7
  solidarity with, 89, 91, 109
  women and girls, 86–7, 89–90
individualism,
  neoliberal focus on, 6, 11, 14–15, 20, 53
  researchers' uncritical valuing of, 17

inequalities,
  growing, 2, 9, 19, 102
  income, 2, 108
  nonprofits' role in addressing, 2, 20, 105, 85
  social, 2, 6, 92
inflation, impacts of rising, 4, 11, 45, 108, 118
insecurity,
  employment, 3, 7, 62–4, 108–9
  food, 4, 6–7, 20, 94, 111, 116
  funding, 7–8
  housing, 7, 20, 94
  neoliberalism and, 7, 10, 14–15, 108–9
  organizational, 7, 62–3, 108–9, 118
  see also poverty
interns, 46, 73, 105

Jäger, Anto, 15
Johnston, Patrick, 75, 83

Keynesian economics, 11, 20

labour, 55, 67
  market challenges, 61, 101, 99, 117–18
  paid, 18, 25, 31, 37, 45, 95
  poorly compensated, 24, 37, 62–3, 65, 119
  precarious, 2, 16, 28, 58–9, 62–4, 109
  unpaid, 34, 45–6, 57, 61–2
  volunteer, 14, 25, 28, 41, 58, 62
Laforest, Rachel, 71, 73–4
Lasby, David, 95, 98
Lasch, Christopher, 15
legal clinics, 43, 81
Liberal governments, 54–5, 75–6, 80

MacDonald, Bruce, 92
managerialism, 13
managers, 65, 99, 106–7
  lack of replacements for aging, 60–1, 109, 118
  precarity of non-profit, 59–60, 63, 91, 108
Manitoba, 52, 87
marketization of services, 2, 10–15, 17, 19–21, 120

markets,
  civil society versus, 14–15, 20, 24–5
  neoliberal logic of, 10–15, 64, 67, 71, 111
  nonprofits' presence in, 24–5, 33, 46, 53, 111–12
  precarity in labour, 2, 15–16, 28, 57–9, 62–4, 101, 109
  private sector, 5–6, 14, 33, 36
  researchers' uncritical valuing of, 17–18
Maytree Foundation, 61, 85
Mendell, Marguerite, 38
Metcalf Foundation, 61, 85, 97, 104–5
Migrant Rights Network, 82
missions, non-profit, 57
  advocacy in, 7, 10, 66, 82–4, 89–90, 110
  driving force of, 5, 23–4, 36–7, 43, 69, 109
  funding challenges for, 27–30, 45, 68, 80, 83–4
  service provision in, 10, 41–2, 66, 69, 110
  social justice, 8, 12n1, 17, 42, 84, 101, 110–12
  as specialized, 29, 35–6, 41, 61, 86–7
modes of control, 13
Mulé, Nick, 70–1, 76, 80
Muttart Foundation, 85

National Survey of Non-profit and Voluntary Organizations (NSNVO), 26–9, 31–2, 48, 74
Native Women's Association of Canada (NWAC), 86
  Sisters in Spirit campaign, 89–90
Neamtan, Nancy, 38
neoliberalism, 20, 53
  civil society counterbalancing of, 10, 14–15, 39, 71, 113
  community impact of, 8, 14–15, 39, 45, 111–13
  downloading of government services, 2, 5–12, 19, 49, 52, 111
  funding impacts, 8, 16, 39, 63–4, 101–2, 109–13

  ideology of, 6, 10–15, 64, 67, 71, 111
  individualistic focus, 6, 11, 14–15, 20, 53
  inequalities and, 6–10, 14–15, 18–19, 102, 108–9
  nonprofits' mitigation of, 16, 24–5, 29–33, 42, 62, 94, 119
  policy impacts, 6–15, 45–6, 51–3, 70–2, 110–13, 116
  restructuring, 7–14, 66, 69–70, 110–11, 114–17
  rise of, 10–11, 51
  state capture of nonprofits, 23, 110
new public administration/governance, 17
new public management (NPM), 12, 67, 96, 108–11
  elements of, 13–14
nonprofits,
  budgets of, 1, 14, 25, 62
  common features of, 22–7, 33, 43–4
  depictions of, 18, 20–4, 43–4, 111
  Indigenous, *see* Indigenous peoples
  strained capacity of, *see* capacity
non-profit sector,
  benefits plans in, 45–6, 59–62, 101, 117
  compensation in, 24, 34, 45–6, 57, 60–6, 94–5, 117
  data deficit on, 25–6, 43, 115–16
  economic contribution of, 25, 28, 33, 46, 56
  gendered work in, 56–7, 61–2
  lack of investment in, 2, 43, 47, 53–6, 94, 101, 116
  objectives and roles of, 10, 15–16, 22–8
  researchers' perspectives on, 17–19, 43–4
  revenues, 30, 38–9, 42, 46–7, 50–2, 93–5, 108
  scope and size of, 4–5, 25–30, 42–4, 46, 74
  tensions within, 7, 18–20, 54–5, 68–70, 74–6, 114
  training, need for increased, 45, 59–60, 105–6, 109

unpaid labour in, 34, 46, 57, 61–2
Nova Scotia, Community Sector Council of, 98, 105; *see also* African Nova Scotians

Ontario,
  community legal clinics in, 43, 81
  cooperatives in, 33–4
  nonprofits in, 93–4, 98–9, 108, 119
  philanthropic organizations in, 41, 88
  see also State of the Sector report (Ontario)
Ontario Council of Agencies Serving Immigrants (OCASI), 83, 93, 99
Ontario Nonprofit Network, 82–3, 88, 93–4, 114
  "decent work" movement, 59–61, 85, 106

para-public sector, 28, 32, 47–9, 57–9, 68
partnerships
  with government, 6, 12–13, 23–4, 52, 69–70, 83
  strategic, 16, 82
philanthropic foundations, 2, 61, 95
  data on, 40–1, 96–7
  private versus public/community, 39–41, 85n4
Philanthropic Foundations Canada (PFC), 39–41, 84–5, 88, 96
philanthropy, 49, 73, 96–7
  non-profit sector mission, 24, 41, 85
  researchers' uncritical valuing of, 17–18
political economy,
  critical approach to, *see* critical political economy
  non-profit sector in, 25–6, 36, 38, 110
poverty, 85
  nonprofits' mitigation of, 6, 10, 20, 36, 94
precarity,
  concepts of, 7, 16, 62–3
  employment, *see* labour
  neoliberalism and, 11, 96
  nonprofits' resilience versus, 7–8, 91, 112, 114

persistent challenge of, 14, 31, 109
Preston, Valerie, 93, 95, 98
private sector business model, 53
  neoliberal orientation and, 12–13
  service provision, 5–6, 33, 62
privatization, 11, 20–1, 52–3
programs, non-profit,
  evaluation of, 2, 5–12, 19, 66–8, 97, 111
  funding for, 8, 12, 52–5, 63–5, 111, 116–17
  neoliberal state retreat from, 11–12, 17
  provision of, 31, 85, 92–4, 97, 101, 105
  volunteers to maintain, 16, 73
Putnam, Robert, 10, 15

QUANGOS (quasi–non-government organizations), *see* para-public sector
Quebec, 33, 76, 87
  immigrant/refugee settlement in, 83, 98–9
  social economy in, 36–9, 42, 51

racism, 15, 91n1, 102–3
  anti-Black, *see* anti-Black racism
  confronting, 4, 43, 82, 103–7, 109
Raven (Indigenous charity), 87
Raven Indigenous Capital Partners, 54
refugees,
  focus on transitional needs of, 2, 41, 77
  service provision for, 3, 42–3, 83, 95, 100–1
regulation, non-profit and charity,
  examinations of, 73, 80, 85
  increasing, 2, 32, 54, 77
  self-, 26
  see also accountability
religion,
  donations based on involvement in, 48, 50–1
  nonprofit/foundation activity in, 27, 31, 40–1
residential schools, 85–6, 88, 104

resilience,
    amid COVID-19: 91, 97–8, 101, 107
    non-profit sector, 7–10, 15–16, 30–1, 68, 109
    portrayals of, 2, 7
    precarity and, 7–8, 91, 112, 114
retirement, non-profit worker, 61, 117–18
revenues, non-profit, 28, 30, 33, 38–9
    methods of generating, 32, 46–7, 50–2
    precarity and, 32, 42, 93–5, 108
risk shift, 10–12
Rodney, Yvonne, 117
Rodriguez, Melanie, 94–5
Roelofs, Joan, 20, 111
Russell, Nora, 35–8

Salamon, Lester, 22–3
service agencies, *see* agencies
services,
    costs to nonprofits of delivering, 2, 14, 45, 64, 108, 113, 119
    demand for, *see* demand for services
    downloading of government, 2, 5–12, 19, 49–50, 52, 111
    funding focused on, 5, 12, 43, 99–100, 107
    marketization of, 2, 10–15, 17, 19–21, 120
    nonprofits' objective of providing, 10, 31, 41–2, 66, 69, 110
    private market, *see* private sector business model
    provision of community, 3, 28–31, 41–3, 82–7, 93–6, 100–1
    social, *see* social services, non-profit
    virtual versus in-person, 16, 49, 95, 98–100, 107
shadow state, notion of, 20, 110–11
Shields, John, 60–1, 65, 93–6, 98
social deficit, 2, 45, 119
social economy (Quebec), 5, 22, 36–9, 51, 56
social enterprises, 51
    budding, 1, 55
    data on, 36–7
    definition of, 36
    funding and revenues, 5, 23, 32, 37

social finance,
    concept of, 46, 51
    critiques of, 32, 52–3, 55–6
    government support for, 54–5
    see also social impact bonds (SIBs)
social impact bonds (SIBs), 54–5
    concerns with, 52–3
social justice, 90, 104
    market-oriented strategies for, 17–18
    muzzling of, 80, 110–11
    non-profit missions of, 8, 18, 43, 101, 110–12, 120
    nonprofits' advocacy for, 16, 19–20, 27, 69–71, 116
Social Planning Toronto (SPT), 94, 101
social problems, addressing, 20, 53–4
social services, non-profit, 47, 53, 68, 76
    amid COVID-19: 93, 107
    funding for, 40, 47–9, 66–8, 82–3
    provision of, 18–19, 27, 31–2, 41–4, 120
    volunteers for, 31, 58
solidarity,
    anti-racist and Indigenous rights, with, 89, 91, 102–5, 109
    non-profit sector value of, 20, 38, 112
Special Senate Committee on the Charitable Sector report, 49, 78–80, 114–15
stagflation, 11
Stanford Social Innovation Review, 18
state, the,
    coercive power of, 12–14, 18, 23, 64–6, 110
    funding, 5, 18, 23, 28, 54, 69–71, 82
    retreat from responsibilities, 2, 5–12, 17, 19, 52, 119
    "shrinking" of, 12–13, 17, 49, 69, 110–13, 119
    see also government
State of the Sector report (Ontario), 28–32, 58, 62
Statistics Canada, 26n1, 27, 57, 74
    cooperatives, data on, 33–4, 42
    non-profit sector categorizations, 32, 42
    Workplace and Employee Survey, 58–9

technology, 38, 61, 81, 101
  nonprofit/charity use of, 16, 48, 72–3, 79, 100
  virtual service provision, 16, 49, 95, 98–100, 107
Tk'emlúps te Secwépemc Nation, 88, 104
Tombe, Trevor, 86
trade unions, 32, 42, 47, 82
Truth and Reconciliation Commission, 88, 104

umbrella organizations, 61, 97, 99
  advocacy work, 69, 77, 81–3, 90, 114
United Nations (UN), 29, 104

voice, 76, 94
  community, 9, 41, 69–71
  non-profit sector advocacy and, 10, 19, 24, 86, 110–16
voluntarism, 27, 40
  civic spirit of, 24–5, 101
  donations based on, 48, 68
  ethnicity/age and, 50, 118
  neoliberal state reliance on, 57–8, 64, 76, 81, 113
  uncritical valuing of, 17–18, 64, 76
voluntary organizations, 22–9, 57–8, 73, 82, 106
voluntary sector, 28, 41, 85
  non-profit sector labelling as, 18–19, 42–3, 73–4
  reports/surveys, 26–9, 31, 33, 57–9, 63, 71–4, 106
Voluntary Sector Initiative (VSI), 26n1, 59, 114
  creation and process of, 71–3
  critiques about, 73–7, 83
  funding, debates on, 71–7
Volunteer Canada, 82, 91–2, 99
volunteering, 1
  economic value of, 33, 57–8
  rates of, 49, 58, 68, 118
Volunteer Management Professionals of Canada, 91–2, 99
volunteers, 4
  accountability to, 14, 45–6, 65–6
  labour of, 14, 31, 33, 57–8, 62, 76, 81
  nonprofits' use of, 16, 23–5, 28, 56–7, 102
social enterprise, 37

Waldie, Paul, 91–2, 99
Ware, Robert, 14–15
welfare state, 8, 12, 20, 69, 111
women, 48
  Indigenous, 86–7, 89–90
  labour in non-profit sector, 4, 56–9, 61, 61–2
  support programming for, 64, 82, 94, 108–9
work, *see* employment; labour

YMCA, 4, 88